ORGANISATION DESIGNS
FROM
START-UP TO GLOBAL

dynamic designs for growth

First published in 2017

ISBN: 978-1-86922-662-6 (Printed)
ISBN: 978-1-86922-663-3 (ePDF)

Published by KR Publishing
P O Box 3954
Randburg
2125
Republic of South Africa

Tel: (011) 706-6009
Fax: (011) 706-1127
E-mail: orders@knowres.co.za
Website: www.kr.co.za

Printed and bound: HartWood Digital Printing, 243 Alexandra Avenue, Halfway House, Midrand
Typesetting, layout and design: Chirene Hughes, Two Red Crows, chirene@tworedcrows.co.za
Cover design: Chirene Hughes, Two Red Crows, chirene@tworedcrows.co.za
Editing and proofreading: Chirene Hughes, Two Red Crows, chirene@tworedcrows.co.za
Project management: Cia Joubert, KR Publishing, cia@knowres.co.za

ORGANISATION DESIGNS
FROM
START-UP TO GLOBAL

dynamic designs for growth

By Michael Bellerby

kr
publishing

2017

CONTENTS

CONTENTS

2

ABOUT THE AUTHOR

Michael Bellerby has been an organisation designer and strategist for more than 20 years in both consulting and line-management roles. This practical exposure to the benefits of a great design and the dire consequences of a poor design has led to ideas that are both innovative and practical.

Mike lives in England after senior consultancy roles in the United Kingdom, Australia and southern Africa. His expertise in business improvement was gleaned through managing change programmes for over 100 organisations in many industry sectors. A fascination with how work is changing through technology and globalisation led to his research into the complexity of work. In 2003, he wrote a booklet on structuring organisations with Martin Lewis, Structuring *Organisations: The Foundation to Support Learning,* and in 2013 they wrote a book on competencies, *The Competency Equation*, which was published by Knowledge Resources in South Africa. He continues to mix the development and writing of work complexity theories linked to organisation design and leadership competencies with a role as a strategist for a large financial services organisation.

3

4

PREFACE

Organisation Designs from Start-Up to Global is the second in a series of three books that aim to empower business leaders and specialists to effectively design organisations that deliver the valuable outputs required by their organisations.

The first book in the series, *The Competency Equation* (published in 2012 and co-authored with Martin Lewis), sets out the factors that define whether an individual is competent to complete an activity of work and, importantly, finds it enjoyable.

Organisation Designs describes how the design of an organisation changes as it grows and the volume of work increases. Through understanding the work an organisation must do, leaders make choices on how to divide work among the different parts of the organisation. This book provides a framework of the options available to leaders, depending on the volume of work. This is important because in larger organisations the choice of design can lead to significant competitive advantages.

The third book in the series will build on a small book Martin and I published in South Africa in 2003 called *Structuring Organisations*. It was written as part of the *Knowledge Resource's Roadmap Series*, and has recently been relaunched. This book links the work an organisation wants to achieve to employee competence through the design of roles and structures.

These three books cover the spectrum of what I refer to as organisation design. Strategy defines what work an organisation wants to do, where this work takes place and who does it, both in terms of a formal position in a structure and the individuals employed. This book touches on strategy, but focuses on where work takes place in an organisation. *The Competency Equation* focused on understanding which individual is aligned to deliver the work, while the third book, covering structures, will link the design of an organisation to how to structure people in an organisation to optimise the value it can create.

Concentrating on the theme of work in an organisation, the books aim to provide a framework of models for leaders to use to help them answer the following questions:

1. What work will deliver value to the organisation?
2. What do we want the organisation to look like in five years' time?
3. To whom does the organisation have to deliver work?
4. Will the design chosen provide the organisation with a market advantage?
5. How many levels of management are needed to deliver the work?
6. How many people do I need in an organisation?
7. Who is the right person to place in a particular role?
8. How does the organisation ensure employees are happy in their work?

This book focuses on the first four questions, while the last two questions were the focus of *The Competency Equation*. Points 5 and 6 will be the focus of my next book, which covers the structures and roles in an organisation.

Every organisation can be simplified into a design model that reflects how it works – this model should, in turn, reflect the design needed to satisfy the work its stakeholders require from it. If the design is too complex for the work required, costs will be high, and if the design is too simple, it will inhibit the delivery of the work.

Organisation Designs is an important book for leaders of organisations of all sizes, as well as their advisors. I believe that when choosing the right solution for an organisation design, the most important factor to be considered is the context of the complexity of the work that needs to be delivered.

Designing an organisation has become a constant challenge for leaders as market forces and internal change lead to regular reappraisals of whether the current design of the organisation will deliver its strategy. This book aims to provide these leaders with the knowledge to assess the appropriateness of their designs.

A new organisation design is needed when organisations grow, merge or consolidate. The range of design options increases with the size of an organisation; and innovative designs to traditional approaches can lead to step changes in costs and efficiency, and generate rapid increases in market share. The design of organisations becomes most interesting in the larger organisations where it can become a competitive advantage. An organisation design is closely linked to strategy. It is both an enabler of the current strategy and reflects the achievement of previous strategies.

This is not meant to be an 'academic' book but rather a guide for business leaders to use to design their organisations. The book is not full of new theories but attempts to pull together existing ones that offer a logical explanation of the progression of designs from a small to a large organisation.

I have found that many books on organisation design list the different models and their pros and cons without explaining how they apply to a growing organisation. This book's approach creates a context for the theories so that a business leader can apply an appropriate theory for adding value to their organisation.

The main consideration of this book is on *where* work is done in an organisation, rather than describe the rather large variety of options for how work is achieved.

The book is divided into three sections. The first section links an organisation's strategy to the activities or work it chooses in order to achieve its goals. Every business organisation encompasses the same basic framework of activities. however, the number and complexity of the activities within this model increases as an organisation grows. Via leadership decisions, an organisation chooses the work that it believes is best for the organisation; thereafter choosing the internal processes or external suppliers that will deliver the work. How successful the work is delivered will be measured by groups called stakeholders who must be satisfied if they are to continue to support the organisation. The last part of this section looks at how the work in an organisation will be delivered – this mainly relates to choosing where to position leadership decision-making, either centralised or decentralised.

Section two focuses on choosing where to source work – either internally or externally – as these choices lead to an organisation's design. The designs are explained in five macro models from the smallest to the largest organisation, with options provided for the designs in these models, depending on the choice of where the work is done. Movement through these five models is dictated through growth in both the quantity and complexity of work in an organisation. Not many organisations grow to a size that requires the most complex designs but the most well-known brands in the world have progressed through many of these models. This section ends with a review of the growth stages of some of these organisations.

Section three provides some thoughts and guidelines on how to design the work in an organisation as well as choosing the right design to achieve this work.

Finally, the factors for success and failure in each of the organisation design models are reviewed.

At the end you will find a section of recommended reading, which lists some of the books I have found useful in developing ideas around designs; however, this is just a small sample of the literature available on this subject.

During the last 30 years I have worked in over 100 organisations designing strategies, implementing operational improvements and radically changing performance. During this period I started an organisation-design consultancy in South Africa, and after returning to the UK, I worked as a strategist for a bank. This experience has reinforced my belief that an organisation design is vital to enable the implementation of effective strategies. I am convinced that an appropriate design can be a significant competitive advantage, just as an inappropriate design can result in the failure of the organisation.

The concepts discussed are straightforward and I hope clear in their potential application. They have been developed through observing real organisations and the descriptions used tested with line managers. I hope you will find that the theories of work, organisation-design models and implementation approaches are useful tools to understand and grow your organisation.

ACKNOWLEDGEMENTS

This publication has been in development for the last 15 years. Fortunately at home I have a very patient and supportive family – Victoria, my wife and guide to whether it is readable, and my children, Kieran and Maeve, who may one day read it too.

This book sits on the back of theorists who have studied organisations for many decades, and who have documented their experiences and observations. While much of this book is not new, it will provide a context for the widely accepted concepts originally observed and noted by these theorists. Without their insights, this book would not have been possible.

I worked with Martin Lewis in South Africa for many years and it was through his inspiration that we challenged conventional approaches to find solutions that worked in Africa. We held many conversations around the complexity of work and its impact both on the design of organisations and the profile of the people who deliver it. With Martin, I was lucky enough to work with many dynamic consultants who encouraged new ideas. Some of these individuals are Lisa Ashton, Karen Dallas, Carl Wagner, Harry and Mellissa Middleton, and Chris Blair.

Two Red Crows Publishing has picked up my rough manuscripts and turned them into books, so a big thank you to Chirene Hughes, Janine Hoek, Wendy Maritz and Lauren Wright; and to Jenny de Wet for the index.

Thank you to Wilhelm Crous, Managing Director, and Cia Joubert, Head of Publishing, at Knowledge Resources in South Africa, for publishing and supporting my previous publications co-authored with Martin Lewis, *The Competency Equation* and *Structuring Organisations*, both part of the *Roadmap Series*.

Finally, I am extremely grateful to my many clients and employers for the opportunity to observe their businesses; these experiences led to the conclusions reached in this book.

AN INTRODUCTION TO ORGANISATION DESIGN MODELS

This book describes the organisation design steps that can take an organisation from a small start-up and turn it into a global giant.

A simple definition of an organisation is "a social group deliberately created and maintained for the purpose of achieving specific objectives" (*The Penguin Management Handbook*, page 361, 1987). This definition is very broad but reflects the fact that millions of organisations exist in the world. Each of us will interface with hundreds of organisations either as a customer, employee, supplier or interested party during our lives. This interface can be fleeting or occur frequently over many years. The organisations may be very large or very small, consisting of two people or up to hundreds of thousands of employees or members.

From earliest times, the basic structure of any society was a simple organisation where people worked together in small teams to deliver a benefit for the broader good of that society. This basic human characteristic hasn't really changed, but as societies became more complex so did their organisations. Think of early governments and armies that were developed during the era of the Roman Empire, for example.

Until the Industrial Revolution, most businesses were simple. But during the 19th and 20th centuries, massive organisations such as Ford, General Electric and HSBC grew to dominate large shares of their chosen markets. These organisations took decades to grow to their current size, but towards the end of the 20th century and the beginning of this one, we have seen a new phenomenon of organisations growing from a simple start-up to becoming a global household name at incredible speeds. A good example of this is Facebook.

The design of an organisation is a picture of the way it chooses to organise the work or tasks to deliver the value it creates. An effective organisation design needs to be as complex as its business objectives. When the quantity of work produced is small, the design can be simple. However, as the complexity and volume of work increases, the design of an organisation becomes more complex in order to deliver it.

Countries have varying strengths in different organisation designs. Although many of the largest organisations are USA-based, Germany has particular strength in medium-sized organisations. It should also be noted that the dominance of countries changes as their economies do. In 1987 Japan dominated the list of largest organisations in the world, with eight in the top 10. In 2009 only three were American, but by 2014 nine were American. The top-10 companies ranked according to market value by Statista in 2014 are as follows:

Apple
ExxonMobil
Microsoft
Google
Berkshire Hathaway
Johnson & Johnson
Wells Fargo
General Electric
Roche
Walmart Stores

Global organisations such as Apple, Exxon and Google have all gone through the same steps-of-growth models. Although each will have chosen a unique growth path, there is nearly always a link back to a person or small team who created a great idea, which grew them into the global organisations they are today. This growth pattern – from an idea to a global organisation – can be classified into five broad design models that can be used to classify all organisations in the world today. Aside from a small start-up – the lowest complexity of organisation design model – to the most complex design model of an organisation, which we term 'global', there are three further organisation design models: basic management, mature business and corporate.

The five model designs described in this book can be classified as macro designs as within them are housed numerous options of more detailed designs from which an organisation can choose. These options include choices for markets, locations, technology, supplier mix, internal processes, company policies, structures and employees. These choices deliver the organisation's performance, create differences between competitors and make each organisation unique.

The most basic model is termed start-up. It consists of a small team of cooperating individuals conducting similar activities to deliver the value-adding work that is the reason for the organisation's existence. Not all organisations have to be formed as a start-up model. It is possible to initiate from scratch a 'start-up' that can be an extremely complex organisation given enough resources. However, for the development of these theories, I will assume that a start-up organisation is a small team of people entering a market for the first time with a new idea for a product or service. At the other end of the scale, a globally dominant organisation could feasibly be a small team of experts leveraging a great idea via technology, but for our purposes we will assume that an organisation that is globally dominant is very large.

In a start-up model, the members of the team share the small amount of management work required in an organisation of its size. This type of model has an entrepreneurial theme as it is the most common design for small businesses, and success at this level can lead to more complex designs.

From this team model, the next architecture stage is to dedicate one or more positions in the organisation to a full-time management role providing two levels of work, namely doers, who create the organisation's value, and management, which coordinates activities and delivers some work for stakeholders. This second model of an organisation is termed basic management.

As an organisation grows, the increased number of workers and/ or the complexity of technology applied requires a dedicated supervisory level and the formal structuring of a dedicated multifunctional management team. In this model, a new level of work emerges – to manage managers. This third type of design, referred to as a mature business model forms the foundation building block for the design of larger, more complex organisations.

Further growth leads to the addition of more business units, which in turn will lead to a need for another hierarchy level of a multidisciplined leadership team in a central head office. The role of the executive team is to ensure synergy across the organisation and provide the strategic services to enable continued success. This fourth type of design is known as a corporate model and it is the most common model for a stock-market-listed organisation.

The corporate model can support the largest organisation if the scope of activities is restricted to a single industry sector. Separate corporate organisations are normally required for each industry sector, especially when the industry is highly regulated, putting specific competency expectations on to leadership roles such as in mining or banking. When it is necessary to direct two or more corporate model organisations, a level of work is required to create long-term synergies from a portfolio of large organisations. This leads to the final and most complex design, which is termed the global model. In this model there is a level of direction and control above organisations utilising the corporate model. This is the model applied in the world's largest and most complex organisations.

The progression of organisation designs from one level of complexity to the next is the result of a successful strategy. To grow a business to a point where it requires the implementation of a more complex organisation design is a significant milestone for that organisation. It should be a goal that is actively managed by leaders with the same level of focus as those for turnover or profitability.

Each of these models has its own characteristics, which are explained in the following pages. These models support a categorisation of organisations, and I have found that over 90 percent of business organisations I have assessed fall easily into one of these models. The 'unclear' organisations were the ones that were transitioning from one model to the next.

Organisations do not necessarily have to grow through these models, and can be formed at any one of the stages. The strategic organisation work design challenge is to decide whether the organisation should stay in its current model, grow to the next model, or possibly move down to the model below. Growth, although popular, is not always the preferred approach as many successful companies, especially in Europe, have found that perfecting their niche in their preferred model brings long-term stability as opposed to the risks associated with growth.

Organisation design is becoming recognised as a key competitive factor in an organisation's success. It is a key leadership competency as the ultimate design decisions rest with the executive of an organisation, normally the CEO.

A leader should be aware of the current model of their organisation, its strengths and vulnerabilities. It is a leadership accountability to implement an organisation design that will deliver its desired strategy. Within a strategy, there should be a clear articulation of whether there is a goal to develop into a new design model or optimise the organisation within its current model.

The models can be used to categorise and compare organisations. They create a comparative lens to review organisations and the work they do. A leader can use them to describe what an organisation looks like now, and what it should look like when a strategy has been achieved. From a more macro perspective, they also provide a theory that can be used to compare organisations in a market or sector to assess the success of design options utilised.

Some businesses start off small, based on someone's great idea, and then grow to dominate an industry or market on a global scale. However, well over 90 percent of all organisations in the world are still at a start-up level of complexity.

As organisations grow and become more complex, with more customers, locations, products and employees, they need to implement organisation design models that match their complexity to get the work done. To 'get the work done' means to satisfy the expectations of the stakeholders of the organisation. As growth attracts more stakeholders, and as each stakeholder requires work from the organisation, more employees are needed who, in turn, require leaders. Leadership numbers increase because every change in stakeholder requirements will require a leadership decision somewhere in the organisation. There is a direct correlation between the number of stakeholders and the volume of leadership work required. As each leader can only manage a limited amount of work, the more stakeholders in an organisation, the more bands of leadership are required. These growing bands of leadership are key to defining the progression through the design models.

Most organisations grow in an unstructured manner, making it up as they go along. Some are successful, but many organisations fail at each stage of complexity. The models provide a framework for growth, and if leaders can recognise the next stage of growth, they can focus on strategies that can get them to the next organisation model.

Many of today's largest organisations have grown through each of these five stages of growth, some in a few years, while others have taken decades. The speed of growth for many is accelerating. A few years ago nobody could have predicted that a company such as Facebook could grow from start-up in 2004 and have a potential market value of nearly $200 billion by 2014.

An organisation design is described both through the models and through the building blocks of design elements that can be used to picture work within an individual organisation. The most important design element is a business unit, as this could be a viable stand-alone business in its own right. Other elements divide up work within a business unit or provide leadership and services to the business units. All elements in an organisation should support the delivery of value from the organisation.

Before an organisation design can be made, the organisation needs to choose the work it wants to do. Organisation work design is the translation of strategy into where work should take place in each part of an organisation. It is the stage before structuring the people in the organisation to deliver the work within the design.

The design is not the business or operating model of the organisation but the framework within which these models work. If there is a large change to either a business or operating model design in an organisation, there is a good chance that the organisation design will also have to change.

The most critical aspect of organisation design is leadership direction and its commitment to a chosen route.

SECTION 1

WORK IN AN ORGANISATION

INTRODUCTION

This section focuses on the first stage of organisation design, which is when the leaders of an organisation choose the work they want their organisation to conduct. Being able to describe work in an organisation enables the development of an organisation design that will deliver it.

An organisation exists to complete activities or outputs that we call work, and this work is hopefully valuable. The type of work is wide and varied, whether it is conducted in a charity, a hospital, an army or a bank. The choice of work will require an initial strategy that further describes the particular intent of the organisation, such as a hospital for children or a digital bank.

This initial choice leads to the work in an organisation, as well as the processes that similarly themed institutions will be required to adhere to, such as the legal entity it must be registered as, and the laws and regulations with which it must comply.

Within these broad parameters each organisation will be unique because it can decide how to deliver the work it has chosen to do. An organisation can choose its location, the processes it wants to apply, the people it wishes to recruit, the customers it wants to attract, the suppliers it wants to use, and the way it wishes to manage its organisation.

These choices lead to stakeholders in the organisation who measure its output and the performance of work. As organisations grow, the volume of work will grow, and with this the number of stakeholders. The challenge of delivering this work is met by the organisation design. A good organisation design will deliver work effectively to its stakeholders.

THE FIRST STAGE IN ORGANISATION DESIGN: AN ORGANISATION CHOOSES THE WORK ITS DESIGN MUST DELIVER

Organisations normally originate from a group of people with a great idea to do something different. This idea may be short term, such as organising an event, or long term, thus potentially creating an organisation that could last hundreds of years.

All organisations deliver some form of work. Part of this work provides direct value to customers, other work is required by legislation, some work creates new opportunities, and other work is needed to protect the organisation from risks.

The reason the organisation exists is to produce valuable work, which can be described as the successful completion of tasks that combine to produce, to the required standard, a valuable measurable output that the organisation's stakeholders require. In a perfect world an organisation would only produce valuable work; however, frequently, work in an organisation has no value – it may duplicate existing work, it may fail quality standards, or its chosen method of delivery may be highly inefficient.

Within this broad definition of work, organisations produce outputs that are hugely varied – from teaching students and fighting wars to treating patients. The main theme in this book is commercial work, which is the foundation of our society. There are millions of organisations doing commercial or business work, including those found in the agricultural, mining, manufacturing and financial-services sectors.

Why the organisation exists can be called its intent. The intent describes the great idea that started the organisation. The intent of the organisation leads to decisions around its legal entity, its strategy, who its stakeholders are, what work it wants to do and how it wants to do it. The initial positioning of a new organisation is to categorise it within a broad theme of work, such as medical, educational, business or government. The intent leads to the choice of legal entity options, and positions the organisation within a chosen sector of the market.

An organisation is a separate legal entity to the individuals in it, so one of the first decisions to make when setting up an organisation is to choose the appropriate legal entity, as some of the rules the organisation needs to comply with will be governed by this decision.

Some of the options for this legal entity are:
- Partnership
- Limited liability company
- Public limited company
- Non-profit organisation
- Government-owned
- Charity
- Cooperative

The choice of legal entity sets the rules and expectations of how the organisation needs to operate, and along with this defines some of the stakeholders interested in its outputs. Once the legal entity of the organisation has been chosen, the work within it can be described using a model that illustrates the activities of any organisation within that sector.

This is called a foundation model and it pictures the minimum activities that every organisation in a particular sector needs to complete, and how these activities link up with each other. In so doing, it provides a framework for understanding the work choices that need to be agreed upon for any size of organisation in the sector. This design challenge will be greater if the organisation is more complex, as the variety of choices for what work to do and how to do it increases with its complexity.

The starting point for design in the model is the organisation's intent. This intent broadly defines the choice of the type of work that will be conducted in the organisation, which is normally an idea to make money. The intent should be succinct enough to be described in a short statement that all employees can relate to. In larger organisations, vision and mission statements attempt to clarify this intent. An intent can cover a vast range of ventures, such as farming a piece of land, opening a restaurant or creating an industrial conglomerate.

Many organisations find that over time they may grow and develop away from their original intent, either because of new opportunities or changing stakeholder demands. This means they need to redefine their organisation's intent as they grow.

How to achieve this intent requires plans, often called strategies. The leaders of an organisation need to choose the route to deliver its intent. This strategy aims to identify the actions required to effectively use the assets available to the organisation to realise the organisation's intent in a given timeframe.

A strategy should:
- Translate the intent into organisation goals and objectives for a time period that is related to the organisation's complexity. These goals will directly influence the organisation's design criteria.
- Be developed from the current organisation position, interpretations of stakeholder demands and limitations set by the quantity of its resource assets.
- Balance goals and objectives across all aspects of the organisation.
- Be contextualized within the complexity of the organisation, and could be termed the corporate plan, business plan or department plan, depending on this context.

A strategy focuses on the organisation's market, and from this analysis guidance is provided on the choices the leaders of the

organisation will make in terms of:
- What products are needed – the choice of product ranges.
- Which markets to sell in – customer locations.
- Who wants the product – customer profiles.
- How to get the product to the customer – the channels of distribution to be used.
- How much of the product will the customers want – product quantities.
- The opportunities of doing work differently to other competitors – the competitive niche that will deliver value to the customers.

To deliver the strategy, the organisation will choose the markets, processes and structures it believes will best meet its needs given the available resources. This choice is often influenced by a particular strength the organisation has in an aspect of its business. This core competency provides its competitive advantage. An organisation may have a competitive advantage through its brand, investment in technology, product quality and the competence of its employees, but having an effective design of the work in the organisation is consistently a major contributor to its success.

Core competencies that provide a market advantage, such as product or process innovation, have been vital for organisations to find the market space to grow from a start-up to a global organisation. Core competencies that may enable this growth include the following:
- **Products** with a worldwide appeal such as McDonald's, Coca Cola and Starbucks, with their Big Macs, Coke and coffee respectively, have many competitor products but they have found *that* product or brand that has an enduring appeal to a broad section of the population.
- **Great customer service** is often linked with other factors, including product. Good examples are McDonald's food and Apple's iPhone.
- **Technology innovation** either at product or process levels, such as the Dyson vacuum cleaner.

- **An ability to leverage a brand** competency from one area into other markets, such as Disney.
- **Financial strength** or access to low-interest capital.
- **Owning a resource** such as De Beers in South Africa that dominates the mining and distribution of diamonds.
- **Monopolies** including Government.

In simple organisations, strategy development may take up a few hours of the leaders' time, whereas in large, highly complex corporate organisations, strategy development and its link to developing new opportunities as well as to protecting the organisation from threats could be the constant focus for large teams within the organisation. The strategies for an organisation can become more complex when there are more resources and increased numbers of stakeholders.

The resources and assets available to an organisation will dictate its choice of work. Resources in terms of the financial investment to be made in the organisation, and the capabilities of its leaders are very important but so are a wide range of other organisational assets and core competencies, such as brand strength, patents and expert employees. The financial resources will dictate the leverage to start a new business and set a limit on its complexity. With only a little funding the organisation will be simple, but with significant financial resources, the organisation formed could be huge.

All organisations will have stakeholders, which are the groups of people or organisations interested in the work the organisation delivers. For any business, the main stakeholder group must be customers. If the business requires materials or services, these will be sourced from supplier stakeholders. Legislative and societal stakeholders will dictate requirements of the business in terms of the parameters by which it is run. Internally, employees will be stakeholders in the business. The final group is made up of financial stakeholders who are interested in the financial performance of the organisation.

Assuming that the business has the resources for its strategy and can satisfy stakeholder demands, it will then have three areas to focus on in its choice of work to deliver its strategy. These are the chosen market, the processes that produce the work, and the structure. Clarifying these elements of the model are necessary for designing the organisation in order to deliver them.

The choice of the market is where the organisation wants to sell or deliver its output. This output is normally described as products. The choice of product and market leads to further distribution or sales delivery channels to customers. These choices of distribution channels can be described as physical assets, for example a shop, website or offices.

To deliver the products to these markets, internal processes are required. Leadership has to choose how to deliver value using the resources available to the organisation. If their chosen processes are competitive and satisfy customer needs, the organisation has a good chance of being successful. Frequently the choice of process will influence the quantity of valuable to non-valuable work the organisation produces.

Physical assets, such as machinery or factories, may need to be purchased to deliver the work, and systems implemented to make sure the work is delivered effectively using these assets.

The market and the processes are useless without people, and the structure dictates how the people employed in the organisation deliver the work needed. The structure is made up of the employees chosen to work in the business and the systems they use to produce output. Once employed, these people also become stakeholders in the organisation. An organisation design aims to deliver the work needed in the strategy and the structure follows this design.

These choices combine to produce the organisation's performance, the delivery of which could be acceptable or non-acceptable to the stakeholders. The performance of the organisation will increase or decrease its assets and the satisfaction level of stakeholders and will, over time, lead to the culture of the organisation. Good performance will lead to increased resources, such as financial resources, which in turn will provide a foundation for growth in the future.

These different elements in the choice of work in an organisation are pictured in the following foundation business model:

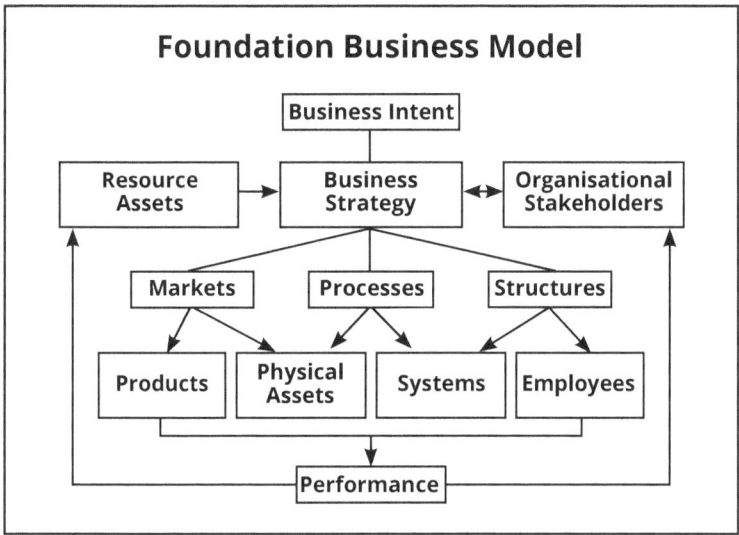

Foundation Business Model

Business Intent

Resource Assets → Business Strategy ↔ Organisational Stakeholders

Markets   Processes   Structures

Products   Physical Assets   Systems   Employees

Performance

An organisation can use the foundation business model as a tool to help design an organisation and to discuss with leaders the choices they want to make in each element of the model. An organisation design reflects the choices made by leaders as to how they want to operate their business.

This model of work in an organisation is the foundation of work analysis in any business organisation from a start-up to a global enterprise. The choices an organisation makes in each of the model boxes dictate the design of an organisation and whether it will be successful. All business and commercial organisations will have some form of activity in each of the blocks in the foundation business model, whether it's a stall in a market or the largest global organisation. A larger organisation with all the elements of the foundation business model is often termed a business unit.

The choice of work in an organisation is based around two major processes of work: firstly, one or more horizontal value-chain processes that transform inputs to the organisation into greater value outputs, termed the customer value chain, which delivers the customer experience; and, secondly, the internal management and support processes. The activities of the customer value chain and the management/support processes need to be coordinated effectively as their combined activities lead to the profitability of the business or value creation for a service. Organisation design can be viewed as the activity of placing management and value-chain processes into a framework that will achieve the strategic goals through satisfying stakeholders.

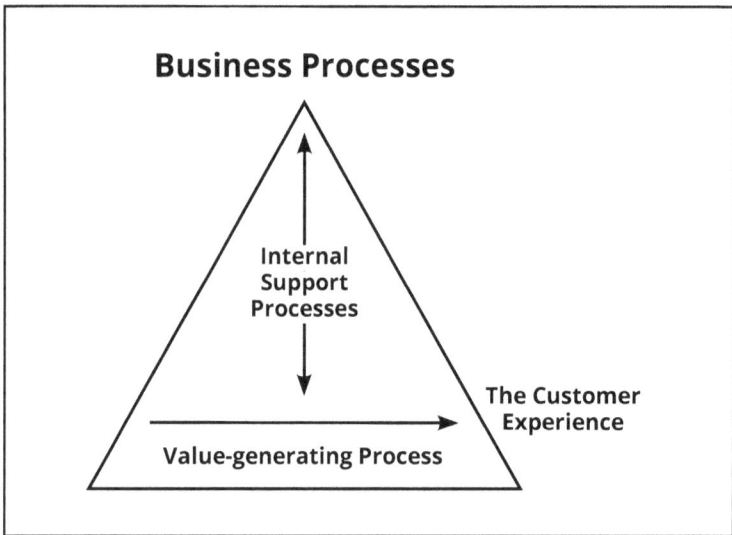

Business Processes

Internal
Support
Processes

The Customer
Experience

Value-generating Process

An organisation has a wide variety of options as to how to deliver work, such as the people it employs, its systems, the technology it uses, how it distributes the services or products and its management practices, to name a few. The leadership of the organisation has a choice of where and how this work takes places. These choices will make each organisation unique.

Customer value chains and their split within the organisation are a major influencer in the organisation's design. A business unit will have at least one customer value chain but may have several. The choice of how to deliver a value chain is the basic criteria of how many business units there are in an organisation. If the value chains have synergies between them, it makes sense to have them in a single unit; but if these synergies decrease or even inhibit another value chain's performance, it could be time to manage them as separate business units.

When defining the processes, it is important from a design perspective to understand the links between them. Some processes are separate from interaction with other processes. Others are sequenced: this occurs when the outputs of one process become inputs of the next process in the sequence. The relationship between the value chain and supportive processes should be one where the outputs of the support processes enable the outputs of the value chain.

Within each customer value chain there will be multiple processes to 'make' the products. Some organisations have multiple manufacturing processes leading to a combination that translates into a single customer product, while others have a single manufacturing process leading to many different customer products.

The choice of internal value chains' processes is a fundamental organisation design decision for each organisation leading to options of the most suitable models for the design. Multiple value chains could support multiple business units, and location splits for processes could support a geographical focus of business elements.

The design of the vertical internal support processes will lead to the choices of where support services and management elements are located in the organisation.

How work is conducted can be classified as the culture of the organisation, including the behaviours acceptable to the organisation. The current culture of the organisation often impacts how and where work should be done. Competitiveness can sometime be gained through challenging a prevailing culture and changing the acceptable behaviours of how work is done in the organisation. As businesses become more complex, the choice of where work takes place in an organisation is largely linked to the prevalent culture of control.

When deciding where work should take place in an organisation, leaders need to balance the pros and cons of centralising or decentralising the accountability for outputs. The amount of centralised control needs to be matched to the stakeholders' needs and the size of the organisation. In smaller organisations the choice is between where to place functional activities in the business, ie within the functional team or within different process-orientated teams.

Centralisation can be viewed as where business-thinking and decision-making reside in an organisation. Strategy, corporate governance and policy-making are normally centralised with leadership. However, the operational management of profitability and the setting of rules on how the organisation works are more variable in their location within an organisation.

If these activities occur in one place in the organisation, it will be highly centralised and probably operate as a single business unit. This approach has the advantage of focused control through an ability to monitor the activities of the organisation. A centralised approach should minimise the duplication of services and reduce the costs of expensive general management leaders. This centralised control provides standardisation but this inhibits variety and the flexibility to change.

A decentralised approach is one that pushes operational accountability for decisions such as profitability out of centralised control and into other elements of the organisation. In an environment that is rapidly changing, a decentralised approach has many advantages, such as closer customer focus and speed of decision-making.

"The need to organize for change also requires a high degree of decentralization. This is because the organization must be structured to make decisions quickly. And these decisions must be based on closeness to performance, to the market, to technology and to all the many changes in society, the environment, demographics and knowledge that provide opportunities for innovation." (Peter F. Drucker, 'The New Society of Organizations', *Harvard Business Review*, 1992)

Highly centralised organisations will tend to be a single business unit but a decentralised organisation will normally have several business units.

It should be noted that many organisations look like they are decentralised with several business units but there is a centralised culture and the business units are really income centres. These income centres might create a calculated profit but they do this through changing price and sales volumes rather than being in control of all aspects of the foundation business model.

Many organisations progress through phases of centralisation and decentralisation that are linked to their growth phases. A young organisation is likely to be highly flexible as it is experimenting to find the best approach to its chosen market. As the organisation grows, challenges of quality control, synergy and the satisfaction of external stakeholders will force more standard rules to be implemented through centralised control. Too much standardisation will lead to a lack of flexibility of the business elements to react quickly to their own markets and so may start to lose competitiveness. This need for competitiveness will drive decentralisation and less standardisation, which will be achieved through pushing some decision-making lower down in the organisation hierarchy.

An organisation may find it beneficial to have greater centralisation when:
- Poor control over the business is impacting the leaders' ability to govern it.
- There are conflicts of interest between business elements leading to a lack of synergy.
- Product or service quality is declining.
- There is large-scale duplication of internal services and activities.
- The variety of systems used makes the consolidation of information and a clear picture of organisational performance difficult to achieve.
- There is a need to provide outputs for bureaucratic stakeholders, such as industry regulators.

Alternatively, an organisation may find that it is beneficial to have greater decentralisation when:
- Competitors are taking market share due to their ability to act more quickly to market demands.
- Key business leaders are leaving the organisation due to frustration from the lack of scope to manage the profitability of their business elements.
- Central standardisation is having the effect of averaging organisational performance rather than applying specific approaches that optimise the potential of each element in the organisation.
- There is a lack of clarity of the performance of different elements of the organisation.
- The work required by some stakeholder groups is not being achieved.

From an organisation work design perspective, an organisation requiring centralised control is likely to resist the creation of more business units, while one wanting more decentralisation is likely to create more business units and service elements.

In many of these examples, the organisation design solution may not be the first or best route to solving the problem. Improving processes, and changes to structuring, technology or behaviour in the organisation's culture may need to be considered.

An organisation is never wholly centralised or decentralised as decisions take place in all parts of the organisation. The quantity of centralised to decentralised control can only be put into context by comparing it with other potential designs or with other organisations. The business environment plays a part in the amount of centralisation or decentralisation, such as the quantity of government regulations.

The quantity of rules and regulations on how work should be done is termed the bureaucracy within the organisation. With too much bureaucracy there is little flexibility and innovative scope in how a business should function.

33

Bureaucracy is often linked to the work an organisation has to do to comply with legislation or regulations. This work is often seen as a cost to the business that adds little value. To some extent, bureaucracy is needed in all organisations as standardisation is required by the stakeholders who set the rules and regulations of how to conduct the organisation. Legislation sets many rules for each organisation, such as accounting standards, payment of tax, the duties of directors and how to conduct the business safely. Non-compliance with these standards will lead to closure of the business, thus too little standardisation leads to high levels of business risk. The larger the organisation becomes, the more likely it will control through bureaucracy.

As organisations grow from a start-up, they need more rules and procedures to ensure that work is done, which results in the trend towards bureaucracy. These rules are normally focused on ensuring the following:

- Corporate governance of the whole organisation
- Conformance to accounting standards
- Policies to comply with legislation
- A standard brand or image
- Quality of products and services
- Effective allocation of scarce resources such as capital
- Synergy across organisational elements
- Setting boundaries between business elements
- Coordinated planning

The function of these rules is to satisfy the outputs required by the organisation's external stakeholders and to ensure that internally the organisation operates with greater synergy as opposed to if each element were an independent organisation.

Bureaucracy tends to lead to standardisation and uniformity, which suggests a high degree of centralised control. The greater the standardisation in products and working methods within the organisation, the easier it is to set rules and procedures for the work. Being able to describe the work in procedures reduces its complexity, and the resulting standardisation should provide increased productivity, improved quality control and reduced costs.

A diversity of products, markets and work methods in an organisation makes it more complex. With this diversity comes a drive for decentralisation to provide greater flexibility in aligning standardisation to the requirements of each element of the organisation.

Decentralised business units can be given a lot of flexibility and little bureaucracy, and apart from achieving financial results and protecting the overall organisation from risk, they can operate and manage their business independently. A decentralised business unit with high levels of bureaucracy would have little scope for change. Franchises are good examples of this in that the governing organisation sets the image, pricing, the quality and work standards, and the products that a franchisee can work within. Frequently the only scope may be the attraction of new customers.

In a large organisation, the amount of bureaucracy may depend on the type of work being performed. Where conformity is necessary, such as in safety and finance, there will be rules, but where more flexibility is required, possibly in sales, there could be less bureaucracy.

Too much standardisation can stifle a business, making it inflexible to market changes and raising costs to uncompetitive levels. Bureaucracy can inhibit its ability to contend with smaller, more flexible competitors.

In some markets and countries, external stakeholder expectations can cause too much bureaucracy, leading to the failure of businesses or the movement of those businesses to less bureaucratic environments.

Whereas centralisation and decentralisation will impact the design of the organisation, the approach to bureaucracy will impact how the organisation works.

Some organisations keep their business simple by choosing to work in only a small part of the value chain and outsourcing the bulk of the work. This approach reduces the number of stakeholders the organisation needs to satisfy. For example, Coca-Cola does not own the bottling or distribution of their products in many countries.

Some work required by organisations has always been outsourced to suppliers. What is different today is that there is now a greater variety of service options from suppliers. Organisations are choosing to outsource parts of their organisation that were once seen as core elements of the business. Recognition can be given to the fact that there are parts of the business they are good at, and parts they are not competitive in. This competitiveness has expanded to the global market where it is important that work is sourced from the best international location.

The choice of suppliers is also dependent on where that organisation is situated. In more developed countries, a wider range of options is likely, whereas in less developed countries this choice would be restricted, often resulting in that organisation having to do more work internally than a similar organisation in a developed country.

The choices of work and the natural split of these processes have a great impact on the choices of design for the organisation. The quantity of work in an organisation dictates its model and how work is split into business units and other elements of business design.

In many organisations the choice of what work to do is very dynamic: new customers and opportunities are constantly being sought and there is a drive to become more efficient and effective in internal processes. Many new organisations grow rapidly, expanding into new markets and developing product ranges, each of which will bring new groups of stakeholders and new challenges to the organisation's internal processes.

The number of stakeholders in an organisation is a good reflection of the complexity of an organisation and the costs required to operate it. It is likely that organisations with a similar number of stakeholder groups will require similar organisation designs and have a similar level of overall complexity.

THE ROLE OF STAKEHOLDERS

Once an organisation has chosen the work it wants to do, it must satisfy the needs of the stakeholders interested in the delivery of that work. To do this, it must put processes, structures and technology in place to deliver the work expectations. Satisfying the variety of work required for stakeholders creates the size and mix of the various work streams across all functions in an organisation.

The way work is structured in order to deliver it to stakeholders is the organisation's design. An effective design will efficiently satisfy stakeholders and be more competitive compared with an inefficient organisation whose design produces too much non-value-creating work. Monitoring how effectively a design satisfies its stakeholders is a key measure for organisation designers. If stakeholders change their expectations for the work to be delivered, it is likely that some aspect of the organisation design will have to change.

The number of stakeholders requiring different work from the organisation is an important factor to design as opposed to the total number of individual stakeholders. Individual stakeholders do not necessarily make the organisation more complex if each stakeholder wants similar work from an organisation. If this were the case, the most complex organisation would be the ones with the most customers, such as Facebook with a billion users.

Stakeholders could be viewed as individuals, but as numbers grow, it is easier to group together the individuals who want the same work from an organisation into a stakeholder group. The complexity of the organisation is closely linked to the number of stakeholder groups wanting different work from the organisation. As organisations grow, they will attract more stakeholder groups, and with this extra work, the costs of running the organisation will increase. This extra cost should also deliver greater income.

Defining what the same work is could be an issue. If it is defined too narrowly, then too many stakeholder groups are formed, and if defined too widely, it is difficult to allocate accountability for satisfying the stakeholders' work within the organisation.

Each stakeholder group requires an organisation to produce work that matches their expectations. If their expectations are not met, then there will either be a negative impact on the organisation or the organisation will be forced to change what it is doing in order to meet these expectations.

Some stakeholders are eagerly sought by organisations as they create value. These value-creating stakeholders are mainly customers. Other stakeholder groups lead to work, which is a cost of doing business, and can diminish value, for example as a result of certain government regulations.

Every organisation can choose which stakeholders to satisfy and this is an important consideration in the choice of work in the organisation. The benefits of satisfying a stakeholder's need must, in the longer term, exceed the costs to the organisation.

Some organisations may choose not to satisfy some groups of stakeholders. These decisions may be part of day-to-day decision-making, for example choosing which customer groups to sell to or defining terms of conditions for employees. Other choices, such as not paying a supplier, could have legal consequences.

The choice of which stakeholders to satisfy is key to the model of organisation design. The more stakeholder groups to manage, the more complex the organisation will be, and the more it will cost to deliver the work to these stakeholders.

Each business organisation is likely to have stakeholders in six categories: one internal (the employees) and five external to the organisation.

The stakeholder categories are:
- Customers
- Financial
- Legislative
- Suppliers
- Employees
- Society

The broad output requirements for each of the stakeholder categories can be summarised as follows:

CUSTOMERS

These are the people or organisations that directly reward the output of the customer experience with money or recognition of services. This makes customers an extremely important stakeholder category for an organisation. Unless the organisation is a monopoly, customers will have a choice of whether to buy from the organisation or a competitor. They will make this choice by assessing the perceived value of the organisation's products or services.

An organisation must produce the right mix of customer-orientated outputs to attract the customers it wants. Different groups of customers may have different needs, so it is important to define the output requirements of the targeted customer groups or groupings.

Customers will use their own perception to value an organisation's output and this puts them into a dominant position to measure the value chains' output. Some of the customer measures of products and services (ie their attractiveness) offered by an organisation include:

- Price
- Quality
- Convenience of location
- Usefulness of the product
- Delivery time
- Comparison to competitors
- Reliability of service

As customers are the stakeholders who produce value for the organisation, they tend to be the primary focus of organisational effort. For smaller organisations with few stakeholder groups, satisfying the needs of current and new customers is the key to survival as even a few days without profitable customers could be disastrous.

FINANCIAL STAKEHOLDERS

To make money over a period of time is the normal aim of a business organisation as this dictates its survival. In this respect, all stakeholders have an interest in the financial performance of an organisation. For some stakeholders, however, the dominant focus is an organisation's financial performance. These stakeholders are mainly the providers of finance to the organisation and they expect a fair return on their investment. Financial stakeholders include banks, shareholders, private investors, government investors and fund managers.

The financial outputs these stakeholders want tend to be loan repayments, tax payments, dividends and capital growth, and they will want to monitor the financial performance of the work in the organisation. This is normally via traditional financial measures of organisational performance such as:

- Return to investors
- The organisation's turnover
- The value of profit margins
- Cash flows
- Future potential for profits
- The amount and value of assets in an organisation

These outputs are used by some of the financial stakeholders in an organisation to assess the comparative worth of the organisation to other investment opportunities. The financial stakeholders from these assessments will either support the organisation in its endeavours, or the investors will choose to move their funds to a more attractive investment and reduce their risk.

The sources of finance to enable growth expand as an organisation becomes more complex. The options change from personal funding when the organisation is starting up, and develops to venture capital and bank loans, and for larger organisations, equity and bonds. The larger and stronger an organisation becomes, the more options it will have for funding, and low-interest funding is often key to enable it to grow larger.

Governments are also interested in the financial performance so that taxes can be levied, and to enable taxes a government sets the legislation that makes them an important legislative stakeholder.

LEGISLATIVE STAKEHOLDERS

Legislative stakeholders set the standards to which an organisation must conform or face legal action. They tend to have an indirect influence on the organisation as the standards or values normally apply to an industry or sector rather than being specific to a particular organisation.

Stakeholders who set these standards include government, professional associations (such as accounting firms), industry associations and banks.

These stakeholders expect an organisation to conform to set standards. Failure to follow the standards will normally lead to fines, prosecution and, in extreme cases, force an organisation to stop trading. The typical types of legislative output an organisation may be required to conform to are:
- Safety and health laws
- Accounting standards
- Environmental standards
- Labour laws
- Tax legislation
- Trade standards

Each of these regulations or standards will add work to an organisation, and in some larger organisations require whole departments of employees to manage legislative-related work. Organisations often see many of these regulations as bureaucratic costs that inhibit the organisation's potential. Governments especially need to balance the quantity of regulation to business costs to ensure that it is attractive to start up and grow organisations in their country.

If a legal stakeholder changes their requirements resulting in new regulations, compliance could change the cost structure of the whole industry, which, in turn, may open a window of opportunity for innovative new designs.

Organisations also set their own legal agreements when they sign contracts with suppliers and employees. These contracts often describe how the work needs to be delivered, and if these rules are not fulfilled, disputes will need to be resolved by legal experts.

SUPPLIERS

Suppliers provide a product or service to the organisation for which it normally pays a fee. As the organisation is the customer of the supplier, the supplier has a choice of which organisations they want to supply to and how they will treat those organisations. Building a synergistic relationship with suppliers can have significant benefits to an organisation's competitiveness.

The supplier stakeholders in an organisation could be resource suppliers offering, for example, materials, parts, people or finance; ideas suppliers such as consultants; or integral business-service suppliers to whom whole processes can be outsourced.

Suppliers normally require an organisation to produce output in a manner that is aligned to its needs. To match these needs, an organisation will be required to deliver work the supplier needs such as linked systems and contract management.

If an organisation does not work effectively with suppliers, costs will increase and service provision will be sub-optimal.

EMPLOYEES

Employees are internal stakeholders within an organisation. The organisation is able to choose each employee, a process that can have a major impact on competitive performance.

The employees of an organisation expect the organisation to do work that enables them to achieve their individual outputs effectively, which in turn creates value for the organisation, and an enjoyable work experience.

In an organisation the employees group of stakeholders will include value-creating teams, supervisory teams, management, technical specialists, as well as many different groups within these broad categories. Each of these groupings is likely to have different expectations from the organisation.

Examples of the type of outputs that employees require from an organisation are:

- Payment for hours worked
- HR administration systems
- The provision of appropriate tools and resources
- Plans and direction
- Effective teams

The size of an organisation is often defined by its number of employees, which is probably a fairer representation of the organisation design complexity of most organisations than the quantity of capital or turnover. However, the number of employees can misrepresent the complexity of an organisation. A simple organisation may have many employees all doing simple, repetitive tasks, examples of which include postal delivery services or supermarkets. A more complex organisation may have fewer employees but these employees manage the output of innovative ideas or complex machinery. This means that the number of employees is not the sole factor dictating the model of organisation design required.

SOCIETY

Society is a broad grouping of indirect stakeholders in an organisation. This grouping includes a mixture of potential stakeholders in an organisation, such as potential employees, customers, suppliers and shareholders, as well as indirect interested parties who will only take notice of an organisation when a specific event occurs.

These indirect interested parties could be the community around the organisation, political pressure groups, religious pressure groups, government departments and non-traditional competitors. The perception these stakeholders have of an organisation should not be negative and, ideally, should be more positive when compared with competitors.

This group of stakeholders does not normally have specific output requirements. They have special interests and only become a stakeholder in an organisation if it works against these interests. Once attracted to an organisation, the interest groups will require the organisation to perform outputs to satisfy their expectations.

Examples of society interest topics could be:
- Minimum wage of workforce
- Age of workforce, ie child labour
- Environmental impact
- Community development
- Hazardous products
- Health of workforce

These issues, if legislated, would fall in the legislation output category of stakeholders, but often an organisation works within the legislation but outside of the expectations of society pressure groups. With the globalisation of activities, an organisation can find that part of its operation complies with local legislation for safety or employment but falls short of the expectations of these criteria in more advanced countries.

The larger the organisation, especially a multinational dealing with different legislation, the more likely the organisation will be to attract the attention of pressure groups. This attention can happen quickly and in an uncontrollable manner, which sometimes has a major impact on the performance of an organisation. Social media can rapidly influence public perceptions, forcing an organisation to take action to rectify them.

Some of the work these pressure groups could expect from an organisation are:
- Community-development programmes
- Expenditure over and above legislation to conform to pressure group standards
- Changes to product ranges or processes to address concerns
- Investment in image building to portray the right perception if the pressure-group perceptions are false

When implemented effectively, these outputs could ease the focus and attention of the pressure groups and the work required will decrease.

Governments can be a societal stakeholder for larger organisations and can influence an organisation's decision-making without legislation. Countries whose governments play a significantly centralised role in the economy can add significant work to an organisation wanting to enter that market.

As an organisation becomes larger and more complex, it will attract more stakeholder groups. A small, simple organisation will have a handful of stakeholders but a global organisation will have hundreds, if not thousands, of stakeholder groups to satisfy. Each group requires different work, which leads to costs and the need for complex organisation structures.

An organisation, at its initiation and at each of its transition points to a more complex design model, has plenty of flexibility in its choice of the stakeholder groups it wants to service.

It can choose the location of its work (which impacts legislation), what work it does, who it sells to, what suppliers to use, how it funds itself and who to employ. However, once these choices have been made, these groups become far less flexible, with stakeholders dictating many of an organisation's activities.

In order to satisfy its stakeholders, the organisation must implement leadership structures, policies, processes, structures and technology to deliver the work required. How an organisation satisfies the stakeholder needs is a result of decisions within the organisation.

Leaders are involved with all stakeholder groups but they are particularly impacted by financial, legal and societal groups, the latter especially can have a big impact on global organisations by way of governmental and pressure-group influence.

All groups of stakeholders are not equal in the work they demand from an organisation: one group may account for 60% of the total work done in an organisation, while another group may simply need a small form completed once a year.

So, stakeholder groups and their requirements should be weighted in any analysis of their impact on the organisation. The complexity of an organisation is related to the number of stakeholders, the volume of work they create, the amount of change they need and the complexity of the tasks required.

If a stakeholder is not satisfied, this can lead to more work in an organisation. Non-satisfaction leads to rework, waste and possibly litigation. This non-valuable work can hugely increase the workload in an inefficient organisation. In designing an organisation the actual work required needs to be modelled even if this reflects this inefficiency.

As an organisation grows, it is often very beneficial to gain stakeholders, especially customers, as income increases in greater proportion to costs. However, if an organisation chooses to deal with too many stakeholders without the benefit of more revenue, then profits will decrease.

Some organisations try to grow too quickly, expanding into new stakeholder groups without having the resources in place to satisfy the work required. An example of this could be to expand into a new country without having the financial resources to effectively fund the venture.

The major changes that an organisation can choose to undertake that will dramatically increase the number of stakeholders in the business and therefore costs are:
- Mergers and acquisitions
- Increasing locations, especially if these locations are international
- Operating across multiple cultural and legislative environments
- Entering new markets or industry sectors

The most successful organisations are often those that manage their costs more effectively than their competitors do, and one way to achieve this is by having relatively fewer stakeholders. Some of the methods to decrease the number of stakeholders in an organisation include:
- Using a few preferred suppliers rather than multiple suppliers who change regularly.
- Having employees represented by a single union.
- Focusing activities in business-supportive countries.
- Outsourcing services.
- Implementing a single IT platform.
- Expanding through franchises.

Economies of scale are a major factor in reducing costs – the organisation produces more without a proportional increase in the number of stakeholders. Big organisations should be more efficient as they should have less stakeholder groups compared with a group of smaller organisations selling the same volume.

The same organisation in different countries may have vastly different numbers of stakeholders and with varying work requirements, depending on how easy it is to do business in that country. Examples of the causes of an increase in complexity to do business can be less support from government, poor legislation, few or inefficient suppliers, lack of support from a community, high cost of finance and a poorly educated workforce.

If the stakeholders want and need change, they put pressure on the organisation to change the work it does. The impact of these changes could have a large or small impact on the organisation. In the most extreme case, if stakeholder work requires the organisation to change to a new way of working, then the whole organisation may have to transform, changing virtually every aspect of the organisation. At the other extreme, a change could be as small as a new simple task for an employee of the organisation. A change in stakeholder demands is likely to impact some or all of the following parts in an organisations: values, vision, strategy, policies, structure, competencies and systems. When there is a radical change in the work, there is often no option but to change the organisational design.

Each step up to a new organisation design model will be linked to a significant increase in the number of stakeholders. The number of stakeholders leads to the choice of the most appropriate design model. A start-up design is likely to have few stakeholder groups – probably less than 20 – but a global design organisation will have hundreds of stakeholder groups interested in the work it produces.

An organisation that is satisfying stakeholder needs will be in a position to grow. This growth is normally typified by a move to a more complex organisation design model. An organisation that is not satisfying its stakeholders will have to improve and prove itself in its current design before it can plan to grow.

SUMMARY

An organisation design needs to be appropriate for the work it has to deliver. The organisation design is a picture of how the organisation chooses to deliver the work its stakeholders require.

In this section a few key theories that are vital for the design of an organisation have been covered. All sizes of business organisations consist of the same basic activities that combine to form the foundation business model. What work and activities fall within each of these blocks in the models are the result of the choices the organisation makes.

When an organisation is formed, it can choose the work it wants to do and this work can be described through value-chain and process models. The initial choice of work leads to the stakeholders who are interested in measuring the delivery of work from the organisation. Once work commences in an organisation the stakeholders dictate the work required, and although an organisation still has a choice of which stakeholders to satisfy, this becomes more difficult. Only when the organisation expands to bring new work into the organisation does it have a new choice of which stakeholders it wants to satisfy.

An organisation that makes the right choices will be more successful than its competitors, therefore delivering performances that will open opportunities for growth. The huge range of process options linked to leadership choices on how the organisation should make decisions make each organisation unique.

An organisation's initial size and complexity will be limited by the resources available to the owners. An organisation with few resources is likely to look like a start-up model but with enough resources a much larger organisation can be formed.

The size of an organisation is normally measured in financial turnover or number of employees. However, its complexity can also be measured in terms of the number of customers, products, markets and stakeholders. The overall size and complexity of the organisation dictates its design.

SECTION 2

DESIGNING WORK

INTRODUCTION

Once an organisation has decided on the work it wants to do and how it wants to do it, this can be pictured in an organisation design. An organisation design picture will show where different aspects of work take place within the organisation, and it can support a strategic analysis of how the organisation needs to change to enable its strategy.

One of the most valuable uses of an organisation design picture is to design a new or changed organisation. By being able to picture different design options, their pros and cons can be described and discussed.

To support the picturing and understanding of organisation growth, there are five broad models of organisation design that reflect how organisations need to adapt their design as the volume and complexity of their work increase. These models are explained in detail in this section, which also includes examples of how designs can lead to a competitive advantage.

The design of an organisation needs to be dynamic as most organisations are constantly changing their stakeholder mix. And as the mix and number of stakeholders change, the organisation design must also change to align to the new expectations of work. This alignment of the organisation design is a key activity of the leadership in any organisation.

A design strategy of an organisation is to either successfully maintain its current design model or enable the organisation's growth to the next model. Being able to explain, using a picture, what an organisation should look like in five years' time, if a strategy is achieved, is a powerful tool to gain support for a strategic plan.

The success of organisation strategies and designs can often only be seen in hindsight, but all globally renowned organisations would have developed through most of these design models.

PICTURING AN ORGANISATION: THE BUILDING BLOCKS OF ORGANISATION DESIGN

Work in every organisation can be described. An organisation design is a picture, a description of where and how work is delivered in the organisation.

Each organisation is made up of building blocks of defined work activity that can be used to describe and design any organisation. I have termed these building blocks 'design elements': the simplest is a team that will be found in all organisations, and the most complex and rarest is the global strategic centre.

There are no universal rules for describing different parts of an organisation. I have chosen the following descriptions of design elements as the building blocks to describe the design options in this book. They do not cover all the elements found in organisations – some will have elements unique to their organisation or sector.

A business organisation exists to create value for its customers. This value, normally measured by profitability, is created by the whole organisation in smaller businesses, but in larger business there can be multiple profit-delivery sub-organisations. A profit-delivery organisation is a viable business that could be split off or sold from the rest of the organisation as it includes activities covering all the elements of the foundation business model.

A business organisation that has all the elements of a foundation business model, I will term a business unit (in some books it is called a strategic business unit). It could be the whole organisation but it could also be part of a larger organisation.

The first three models of an organisation design described in this book are characterised by having one business unit, while in the final two levels there are more than one business unit.

As a business unit is where a business organisation generates profit (or service value), it is the most important building block in any organisation design. It is key because it provides the organisation's value and is the reason for its existence, whereas other parts of the organisation generally support these activities. One of the most important leadership accountabilities is to decide how and where profit (value) is created in an organisation. If profit is only calculated in one place in the organisation, it will have one business unit; if there is more than one point of profitability measurement, there will be several business units.

General Electric has defined its criteria for a strategic business unit (SBU) as the following:
- it must have a set of external customers. It must have an external, rather than internal, market;
- It should have a clear set of external competitors it is trying to beat.
- It should have control over its own destiny: decide what products to offer, how to obtain supplies and whether or not to use shared corporate resources, such as R&D.
- It must be a profit centre with performance measured by its profits.

The first task of organisation design is to define the business unit or units in the organisation. The design of a business unit can be simple, ie a small team, or it can be a complex organisation with thousands of employees. Once a business unit design has been agreed upon, all other elements of the organisation, such as head offices, service centres and project teams, can be designed as they only exist to enable the business units to be effective. Some elements will fall within a business unit and, in more complex organisations, some will sit outside of the business units.

In a business unit there will be one or more teams, and as the unit grows these teams will be structured into income and cost centres.

A team consists of a few employees either of the same discipline or multidiscipline who are grouped together for common tasks. This is the basic building block found in all organisation designs. In complex organisations there could be thousands of teams delivering the work the organisation needs.

As an organisation grows, teams grow and multiple teams become departments, either with a revenue, service or leadership focus. Departments are normally groups of teams with either a functional or process role. They are led by managers whose role is to deliver the work required by the department's stakeholders.

Another element is a revenue department, sometimes called an income centre, which generates revenue and value from the sale of products and services to customers. The departments are part of a business unit and normally have a functional title such as production or sales. This income-generating element is normally led by a functional expert rather than by a multidisciplined team and these managers rely on support and management services from the rest of the business unit. Direct costs associated with the manufacturing of products or service delivery are normally allocated to these departments, and the income created is viewed as a contribution towards profits. The profit for the overall business is measured centrally in the business unit.

Larger income centres are more difficult to differentiate from a business unit. One of the tests of whether this element is an income centre or a business unit is by assessing how easily it could be sold to an external buyer. A business unit would be easily split from the larger organisation as it would have its own multifunctional leadership team, dedicated systems for its core activities, employees and technical resources creating its valuable output. It will have its own management information systems to reflect performance, dedicated distribution channels and a segmented customer base. An income centre would only control some of these activities.

One of the key factors in defining whether a part of a business is a business unit or an income centre is whether the leaders in that element can make decisions on the price of products sold so that the income achieved will deliver the strategic goals of the unit. This is not tactical pricing to achieve incremental changes in sales volumes. An income centre setting prices will tend to do so to achieve its targeted sales volumes: however, it will not have the insight to know whether this price is best for the overall profitability of the business. A business unit should make pricing decisions based on delivering the return on capital or equity required from a business after all costs and investments have been factored in. Setting and changing this fundamental price level is probably one of the most strategic decisions a business can make.

Service departments, which are sometimes called cost centres, are departments that support the delivery of value from the income-producing elements. They are normally headed by a single functional expert manager rather than a multidisciplined team. These departments normally do not generate revenue but support value creation in the income-generating centres. They are a cost in the calculation of profitability. These departments cover all functions within an organisation that do not produce income or direct value for customers.

A management centre describes the location of the leadership of the whole business unit and possibly some of their support services. This centre can be viewed as a type of service element.

A business unit could be one team but it is normally made up of a number of elements, for instance teams, departments and overall management, as shown in the following graphic:

Examples of Elements in a Business Unit

```
        ┌──────────────────────┐
        │  Management Centre   │
        └──────────────────────┘
          │                  │
┌──────────────┐    ┌──────────────┐
│   Income     │    │   Service    │
│  Department  │    │  Department  │
└──────────────┘    └──────────────┘
      │                    │
┌──────────────┐    ┌──────────────┐
│    Teams     │    │    Teams     │
└──────────────┘    └──────────────┘
```

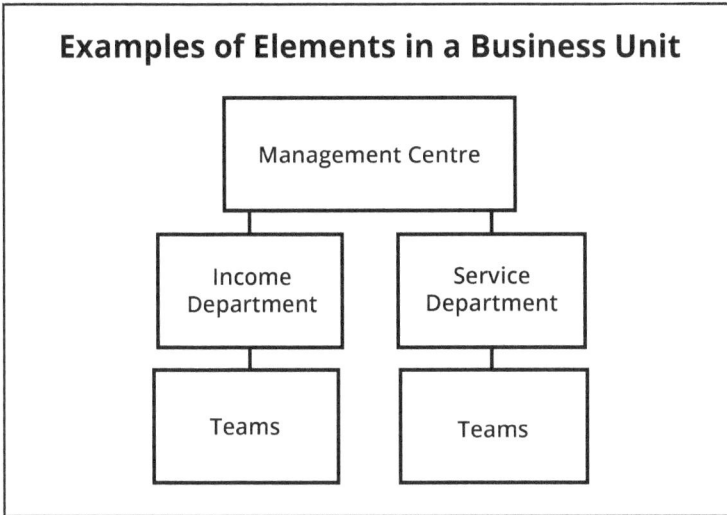

When an organisation has more than one business unit, most organisation designs include further building blocks of design to support the business. The main elements to a more complex design are described below.

Service unit: This is a large service centre supporting multiple business units. It normally includes several different service-centre departments. Examples could be a centralised training centre or research-and-development laboratory. The unit is frequently managed by a multidisciplined team and could be viable as an independent service business to multiple clients if it were not part of the larger organisation. Some service units are allowed to contract for external business, which moves them towards becoming a business unit.

Project units: These are sometimes found in large organisations when there is a need to deliver change or one-off customer solutions. These units will have teams and departments delivering change projects across the whole organisation. They are often less stable than service units as the scope and variety of projects dictate their function, lifespan and resources.

Corporate centres: This management element sits above a number of business units to lead and direct synergy and performance across the units. They are normally closely linked to strategic departments and some service provision. This centre is frequently termed the head office.

Integrating units: These are required when the number of business, service and project units becomes too large or complex for the corporate leadership team to direct and manage. Integrating units further divide the business into groups such as divisions or regions. Some services required by these divisions are normally also located in these units.

Strategic units: These are service units that provide services of a strategic nature for the whole organisation and will include several teams or departments each delivering work in a strategic function. They are normally only found in the largest organisations, possibly in a corporate centre. These services will build or protect a future organisation from risk.

Global strategic centre: This leadership element has a directional role but no management accountability. It sits above a number of corporate centres and is typically structured as a small team of global leaders with some strategic services. This is the rarest of design elements, as it is only required in a few of the largest organisations.

Note: These descriptions of design elements have worked well for me; however, there are many varying definitions and even concepts, such as head office and business unit, which can be described differently by other theorists and within individual organisations.

In designing an organisation with these elements, the final picture will show how the chosen elements are grouped together. Elements in these pictures are normally shown as boxes and joined by lines that indicate reporting links to management centres, integration units or corporate centres. If the organisation is complex, there could be several pictures: at the top level only the largest elements are pictured and then more detailed pictures of the elements within each of these large elements are represented. The top-level picture showing the management structures, groupings of business and services units and the departments that make up each of these units could look like the model below.

Different Elements in Organisation Design

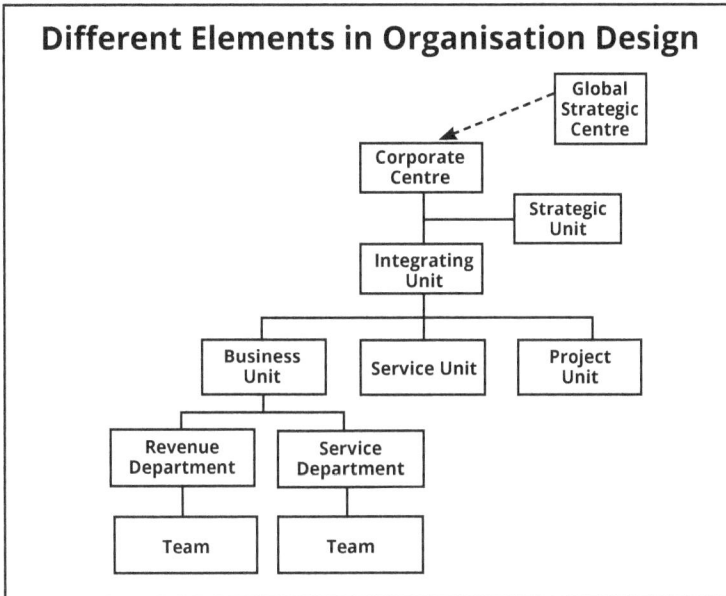

This picture reflects a high-level organisation design of where work is placed in an organisation. Pictures like this one, showing each element of an organisation, will be the output of an organisation design project. They will need to be supported by a high-level description of the philosophy behind the design to make them meaningful to employees and other stakeholders. This description should cover the following:

- Why this design is believed to be the best fit to deliver the organisation's strategy.
- What is the role of each element in the design and what work falls within each of these elements?

- The role of the central functions and where leadership accountability is placed throughout the elements.
- Any changes to the current provision of services for the organisation, such as a new approach to outsourcing and services brought into the organisation and therefore not shown in the pictures.
- Possibly a description of the planned growth areas in the design.

The delivery of work in an organisation will require the design to be supported by business and operating models of the organisation. These models integrate the design with the technology, processes and systems in each specific organisation.

A business model of an organisation describes how the organisation creates value. It summarises the market the organisation wants to service and which customers in this market will be important to it. In order to satisfy these customers, the products and their pricing approach need to be detailed. This normally leads to a comparison with direct competitors, identifying the differentiation of the organisation in its chosen market. The sale of products will create the revenue flow and the business model will explain the profitability of the organisation through comparing this revenue with the overall costs of the organisation. A large element of a business model will be the financial pictures of the organisation in terms of profit and loss (P&L) and balance-sheet projections, probably forecasting several years of performance.

In an organisation that is changing its organisation design, the main benefit of the business model will be to explain the alignment of the design to its strategy. This requires a description of how the organisation is changing in terms of new markets, customer segments and products, and the impact these will have on the commercial performance and design of the organisation. The business model should at least describe the 'Markets' box in the foundation business model. (Please refer to the 'Foundation business model' in Section 1, page 30.)

An operating model of an organisation will describe how the organisation will deliver the customer proposition to create the value detailed in the business model. This model will describe all the processes in the organisation required to deliver the work. Some of this work will sit within the value chain and some, as described earlier, in the internal support processes. The model will explain how work is split into each element and how it is coordinated in the organisation – from central functions down to business units, departments and teams. It should include details on the geographical location of the work, the role of each element in the business design and which work will be sourced externally from the organisation. An important aspect of the model will be how the IT infrastructure will link all the elements of the organisation.

Organisation design pictures are normally a key part in explaining the operating model. In some operating models, the culture and policies that make the organisation different to competitors will be described. This is especially important in a more commoditised market with little differentiation in product or price. If the organisation is changing, the processes impacted by this change should be explained in this operating model. This should support the explanation of why the organisation design is appropriate. The operating model needs to at least describe the 'Processes' box in the foundation business model. (Please refer to the 'Foundation business model' in Section 1, page 30.)

The business and operating models will define the choices made for work required in the organisation and this will lead to the design of roles and technical processes to deliver this work. In addition to these two models, an organisation design will need to be supported by a people structure that pictures the roles required in the organisation to deliver the work the stakeholders need.

A key part of the people structure will be the leadership teams for the organisation. These teams are important elements in any design, as the most senior teams have legal accountability for the performance and governance of the organisation. As organisations become more complex, so too do the leadership team structures, with more roles and more hierarchy levels. The ultimate accountability for decisions made in most commercial organisations is taken by its board.

What is a board? It is a team of directors who jointly oversee the activities of an organisation. The legal responsibilities of the board vary with the type of organisation. The directors are legally accountable to represent the owners of the organisation who are the share or stockholders.

Normally, executive and non-executive directors sitting on a board have accountability for the governance of an organisation. Some organisations legally separate different parts of their organisation, with each part requiring its own board. The challenges of operating in different industries or in countries with cultural differences in legislation frequently lead to multiple board structures. A board is an important element in a design as it is the highest level of leadership accountability in an organisation.

The design elements described previously are the building blocks to picture a specific organisation, and organisations can be categorised within one of the following five broad models of organisation design.

THE FIVE MODELS OF ORGANISATION DESIGN

Five models of design can be used to illustrate how the design of an organisation changes as it grows and becomes more complex. These broad generic models provide a framework to understand the organisation design options for any organisation.

1. The **start-up model** of an organisation is the most basic. It is a team structure where the effective setting up of roles will be important as the individuals play a critical part in achieving success for the organisation.

2. The next is the **basic management** model, in which a dedicated management layer separates out from the teamwork of the start-up model. An organisation needing this model will be moving towards dividing work up into teams or small departments. In this model an appreciation of where work needs to take place in the organisation is required.

3. The **mature business** model is a single business unit with a dedicated multifunctional leadership, coordinating multiple teams in income and cost centres. There will be at least one band of management supervision between the leadership team and the value-creating teams.

4. The **corporate** model is needed to manage multiple business units and the services they require. In this model there are many design options and it is at this stage where an effective organisation design can deliver substantial competitive advantages.

5. The rarest and most complex model is the **global** model. Leadership lies in a global strategic centre that directs a number of corporate model organisations.

Defining the business units in an organisation is an important factor for these models, as a business unit is the key building block. In the organisation design models, 1, 2 and 3 are all single business unit models, whereas 4 and 5 are multiple business unit models.

The models build on each other so that a more complex design is comprised of the less complex models. This means that in using these models we can also break down a large organisation into its constituent parts and start to define the challenges faced by each part of the organisation.

These models are important for benchmarking purposes, as you would normally benchmark organisations with a similar organisational model as they have similar characteristics.

The five different types of organisation design model are pictured in the following table:

LEVELS OF ORGANISATION DESIGN COMPLEXITY

Level of design complexity	Model	Number of business units in the design	Minimum number of hierarchy bands of work	A description of the model	Pictures of the models
1	Start-up	1	1	A team of colleagues without a dedicated management role that coordinates activities to deliver valuable work to a small number of stakeholders.	
2	Basic Management	1	2	One or more dedicated management roles directing the work in at least one value-creating work team.	
3	Mature Business	1	3	A dedicated leader supported by a multifunctional management team. Each leader in this management team manages their own teams to deliver the relevant work required by the various stakeholders with the support of supervisory/ middle managers.	

4	Corporate	At least 2 business units	4	A centralised leadership team directing the activities of at least 2 business units each based on one of the lower complexity models.	
5	Global	Multiple business units within at least 2 corporate models	5	A global centre providing strategic guidance to at least two corporate model organisations.	

KEY

Leader	
Team	
Global strategic centre	
Business unit	
Corporate model	

MODEL 1: START-UP

I have termed this first model of organisation design a start-up organisation. A start-up model is the simplest form of organisation design; it is a single business unit consisting of a small group of individuals working together as a team to achieve common goals.

How many people do you need to call an entity an organisation? It is definitely more than one, and to be called a social group it probably implies three or more individuals. While sole traders and cooperating individuals are extremely important for the economy and often the starting point for many organisations, only when employees are recruited would they progress to this first model of organisation design.

A start-up is the result of an entrepreneur who has a good idea on how to earn a living by owning their own business. Many people prefer the opportunities of working for themselves or in a small team compared with working for a larger organisation.

In most countries it is relatively easy to start a business with the provision of government incentives and the fairly simple paperwork involved in registering a new business. The first challenge for the entrepreneur will be to resource the organisation to develop the good idea and implement value-chain processes to deliver to customers. Starting-up means implementing a strategy, including choosing the market to work in and customers to service, agreeing on team roles, recruiting the first employees, and putting in place the processes and infrastructure needed to deliver the desired strategy.

The majority of business organisations fall into this category and many have been happy with this model for decades, having no ambition to grow further. It is the traditional model for many types of organisations, such as farms, independent local shops, repair services and medical practices. Setting up a legal company with limited liability provides some protection of personal assets compared with being self-employed.

Millions of people work in this small team model. The team delivers several outputs, and the activity within these teams can range from being the most simple to the most complex. This team model is also the basic organisational building block for all larger organisations.

This business model is most frequently located in small offices, laboratories, factories or shops. However, less formal start-up locations have led to some huge global organisations. Facebook started off in a university hall of residence, and Google, Microsoft and even Disney began their ventures in garages. In retail, both Marks and Spencer and Tesco can trace their start-up organisations back to market stalls.

The main criterion for this model is that there is not a dedicated management function. There will be owners or leaders in this organisation but creating value will be a substantial part of their role. All employees do multiple tasks with the main focus being on selling to and servicing customers. Specialist advice to set up and run the organisation is bought in from suppliers, such as legal, accounting and human resources advisors.

This model does not work for an organisation requiring a large number of employees, and will normally have a maximum of 20. It will have a simple, flat structure, consisting of individuals working together as a team to achieve the outputs, without a formal hierarchy or demarcated roles. Activities will be split by competency and experience with all members working as a single team performing the tasks needed at any point in time. The owners and entrepreneurs play a crucial role in generating value for the organisation through the hands-on delivery of services, products and sales. As the owners have invested in the business, they make the final decisions (and also have the most to lose if the business is unsuccessful). This informal structure will also mean that the business-management systems will be very basic, although technical systems required for output could be highly specialised.

Some supervisory and basic business skills are required by the owner or manager of the business. The individuals in these organisations usually do not require high levels of business competencies but rather possess the skills to satisfy customer needs and deliver a profit. For many organisations the work is repetitive and not complex; however, the work of some organisations in this category could be highly complex such as a consultancy or financial advisory practice.

The barriers to entry for this type of organisation are small as the start-up costs are generally low. Success depends on the skills of the individuals. These organisations tend to rely on the quality of their work or product for their competitive edge. The quality of products and services can differentiate a small trader from a larger organisation through offering a unique product. This uniqueness should offer a margin premium that can offset any cost disadvantages of this model.

The simple model will also mean the likelihood of many competitors, but this does not necessarily present a problem as the customer base is often localised. Some large organisations have found that utilising this model to distribute products through multiple small outlets, each manned by a team, can be very successful. A typical example of this is the coffee shop scenario. Starbucks, for example, discovered that it could have multiple simple outlets in close proximity to one another if potential customer flows were different for each outlet.

Because these organisations are small, they will have fewer groups of stakeholders requiring work from the organisation, normally less than 20 groups. A group of stakeholders is a term for all individual stakeholders wanting the same work from the organisation such as all customers buying the same product. A group may be made up of one stakeholder or thousands. The complexity of an organisation is more a factor of the variety of work required by stakeholders than the number of stakeholders.

The stakeholders will include at least one group from each type of stakeholder group, being customers, employees, financial, legal, societal and supplier stakeholders.

Most of these organisations will need to have a continual stream of sales to survive, and it is unlikely that many could survive for longer than three months without an income. Measurement of performance has to take place at least weekly so that sales variations can be addressed immediately. From an investment point of view, this makes the organisation high risk.

This risk is associated with the vulnerabilities of this type of organisation, which include:
- The possibility of key individuals being unable to deliver the required work due to, for example, illness.
- The likelihood of fewer resources, particularly financial strength.
- The immediate effect that poor-quality work will have on results.
- High levels of competition from similar or more complex organisations.

Many organisations in the start-up model fail, and this failure can be rapid as organisations of this size are not resilient to changes in the market. Success may be reflected by long-term survival or the growth of the organisation to a point where it needs to transition to a more complex organisation design.

TRANSITIONING FROM START-UP TO BASIC MANAGEMENT

If the start-up model is successful, as indicated over a period of time, stakeholders will be satisfied, performance will be delivered and business assets will grow. A key factor to this growth is financial strength, either from retained profits or investment. Cash-flow management is particularly important to ensure that the business does not run out of cash while it invests in growth. For the majority of registered businesses within a start-up model, maintaining financial strength means success and there is no desire to grow further. This size of business is enjoyed by many small business owners as it is hands-on, flexible and focused on the delivery of value to the customer.

The initial, dominant focus of any small business is to sell their services and/or products, grow their customer base and increase demand for their products. Without customer demand, the business will fail, but with increased sales, more employees can be hired. With a larger workforce, roles become more demarcated as the volume of activities means there is less multitasking, and as the business grows it requires more management tasks to keep it functioning

As the number of management tasks increases, one or more of the start-up leaders needs to move into a management role removed from the team and hands-on delivery of value. This role will be very different, requiring management competencies to plan, coordinate and control the work in the business, and ensure that the business supports the work outputs required from its growing number of stakeholders.

As leaders in a start-up organisation can choose their own job titles, many start-up businesses may appear to fit into the more complex basic management model, especially if the leader calls him/herself the managing director or a similar title. The test will be in the type of work these leaders do on a day-to-day basis, and if the majority is hands-on value delivery, it is likely to be a start-up organisation model.

If the business idea is good and sales rapidly increase, some businesses have to transition to the more complex basic management model within a few weeks of start-up but for many it takes much longer for this transition to occur.

MODEL 2: BASIC MANAGEMENT

This model has two levels of hierarchy based on at least one dedicated management role leading a team of value-creating employees. This is a slightly more complex organisational structure from model 1. It can be the structure chosen to start a new organisation, but it is often formed when a start-up organisation grows and requires at least one dedicated person, who is often the owner, to complete the management work. The number of employees in this type of organisation is normally small – from 15 to 100 people – depending on the outputs required from the organisation.

A team with less than 15 employees is unlikely to generate enough income and management activities to justify a dedicated management role. The theme of this model is basic management as it is the first design where dedicated management and functional roles are found in organisations. The barriers to entry are still small, but normally require a little more finance and other resources than start-up model organisations. It is likely that there will be fewer groups of stakeholders in this size of organisation, normally less than 40.

As organisations grow they tend to become more secure. This security is based on more customers and more financial resources. As the number of customers increases, the loss of a few has less impact, while growing profits should provide some reserves for downturns in the market as well as a source of capital to grow. This means that leaders can take a longer view of performance, moving from the day-to-day, week-to-week sales focus of the start-up model to monthly plans and building up to annual performance. This enables longer-term investment decisions, and with a performance history it becomes easier to access external funding, for example from banks.

Success in this model is mainly dependent on continued growth in market share, attracting competent employees, achieving good margins on prices, cash-flow management and the enthusiasm of a single or small team of managers.

The vast majority of workers in this size of organisation will be delivering the organisation's chosen value chain – from sales through to either manufacturing and distributing products or delivering a service. These workers will be split up into teams as the organisation grows, with some functions becoming more specialised. These functional requirements of the organisation's value chain include sales, production, service distribution and administration. With more employees, teams similar to the start-up model will start to form and create their own identities within the organisation

The work relationship will consist of a hands-on management approach, with the manager knowing the names and roles of each individual in the organisation. Only the dedicated manager will see the full picture of the organisation and its performance, so they are at the centre of decision-making. The key roles for this leader are to ensure the sustainability of the business and – if desired – to grow the organisation towards a mature business model.

If the organisation has grown from a start-up model, the entrepreneur with the original great idea is normally the person who moves into the leadership role in this model. This can lead to failure if this entrepreneur has poor management competencies and is unsuited for this role.

A lack of expert skills across the functional disciplines required by a business is a risk for this size of organisation. This model buys in the functional expertise it needs when it is required but these services tend to be reactive rather than proactive. For example, an accountancy firm may compile annual accounts or monthly ledgers for the organisation but financial expertise may not be available on a day-to-day basis. This potential lack of indepth expertise can put the organisation at risk compared with its larger competitors.

The focus of systems and technology in the organisation will be for sales and the delivery of the specific products and services. More general systems for financial control and management information are likely to be more basic.

Larger, more complex organisations can be a threat to these organisations. For example, in the UK 'Out of Town' retail centres have led to the closure of many small retailers and traders on local high streets as they couldn't compete with the economies of scale from the larger competitors. A localised market can be both a strength and a weakness for these organisations – the customer base may be loyal and supportive but it is often too small to allow for the economies of scale that allow prices to be set at the same level as larger competitors.

The expansion of many small businesses has traditionally been restricted to the size of the local market and direct competitors. For many of the organisations in this model, the internet offers an opportunity to vastly increase their potential customer base and information technology has opened up opportunities to radically change the design of how these organisations can operate.

Modern technology is having a dramatic impact on the design of many small organisations. The application of technology can transform a simple organisation into a much larger and more complex one. Internet shopping can remove the need for physical locations, such as shops, and the electronic transfer of data or communications means that an accountant in India can be used by an American company.

An organisation linked by information technology is sometimes termed a virtual model and it operates through networking suppliers of services. This means that a relatively small company in terms of assets and employees can generate a huge turnover.

In a virtual organisation model, the individuals within a structure do most of their work away from the organisation and normally have home offices from which they operate. The organisation frequently has a hub structure that coordinates activities, provides standards and procedures, manages information collation, and presents a company image to stakeholders. The individuals work independently but within set rules. This model has been applied in small consultancies but it is also seen by larger organisations as a method of reducing office overheads, providing employees who create value from their knowledge with more flexibility, and a way of expanding to new geographical markets. The model does have its downsides, ie creating a common culture and ensuring quality control become more difficult. In start-up and basic management organisations, this virtual approach has seen substantial growth and may become a dominant business model as it is an efficient model for small teams but its downside can outweigh its benefits as the organisation grows.

TRANSITIONING FROM BASIC MANAGEMENT TO A MATURE BUSINESS MODEL

The transition from a basic management model business to a mature model is gradual, and is a reflection of the growth of the business leading to more employees and dedicated services. When the size and complexity of the business becomes too much for one person to manage effectively, more leaders must be employed, which starts to build a management team.

The growth of a management team leads to functional specialisation in this team and the development of departments to support these functions. Growth leading to functional specialisation is the change driver moving the design from a basic to mature model. The most common initial functional teams are production/service, sales, distribution, finance, human resources and information technology.

In smaller organisations the challenge is not whether to centralise or decentralise but whether to insource or outsource the work. As organisations grow, they tend to insource work from suppliers to be more cost-effective and gain greater control over the activity. This insourcing creates functional teams and departments – the leaders of these teams create a multifunctional leadership team above work supervision and value-creating levels that characterise a mature business unit model.

Moving services in-house is more cost-effective: a smaller organisation may use the services of an internal bookkeeper for monthly records and outsource annual accounts to an accounting firm, whereas a larger organisation employs an accountant to provide dedicated financial advice, manage the bookkeeping teams and complete accounts.

As the organisation grows, the roles of senior employees in each function start to develop into management roles, planning, coordinating and controlling the work of subordinates rather than the delivery of it. This initially creates a supervisory level, and with further growth a management band above supervisors that develops into a leadership team supporting the managing director. With more levels of management, formal communication channels need to be implemented to ensure a cohesive team. Performance may not be observed by the leaders but will need to be monitored through information and key indicators provided by dedicated management and controlled information systems.

This growth to maturity is reflected by the development of dedicated functions with their own processes. Decision-making becomes split into functional decisions and centralised management team decisions. Professional management becomes more important than the ownership of the initial entrepreneurial idea and the bond between ownership and organisation management becomes weaker.

MODEL 3: MATURE BUSINESS

A mature business model is a multiple-department version of the basic management model. Work is split across a wide range of functional teams, some of which will deliver income streams, while others are cost centres supporting the delivery of the value chain.

It is a single business unit, characterised by a single point of profitability for which a general manager – often termed a managing director (MD) – is accountable for the delivery of performance results to the shareholders and other stakeholders. The MD will be supported by a multidisciplined management team, each of whom has departments below them within which are supervisory/middle managers leading teams who create the organisation's value or provide services required by the value chain or other stakeholders. The individuals in the management team have two areas of focus: firstly, to jointly manage the overall value chain's performance and the expectations of all stakeholders in the business and, secondly, to be responsible for managing the processes within their individual disciplines.

The basic structure of this organisation will have three core bands of work below the MD: a dedicated management team that needs to be able to manage managers; then, due to the number of people in the organisation a supervisory management level; and finally a band of value-creation and functional support workers. The actual number of levels of hierarchy below the MD in this complexity of business unit is frequently more than three depending on the complexity of the organisation. The systems required by the organisation will need to be integrated and multidisciplined. It is called a mature business unit because a single business unit does not become any more complex than this model.

It is rare that this complexity of model will be an initial design for a completely new organisation. This design frequently comes about through the growth of a basic management organisation or the merger of two basic management organisations into a single, more complex organisation. The major criterion for this design is that the previously ad-hoc functional specialists are now required on a daily basis and so a dedicated multidisciplined management team is needed to run the organisation.

To support such a management team, the organisation must be large, normally with between 100 and 1 000 employees and also large amounts of mechanical or physical assets. Within this unit there will be elements that are revenue centres and service centres, each made up of several different teams delivering work. These centres are normally split by functions.

This complexity of design within the organisation makes the barriers to entry larger and the number of similar competitors are less.

Although all organisations up to this model with limited liability will have accountable directors and board members who have legal responsibilities such as needing to meet at least once per year to sign off accounts in smaller organisations, ownership is mainly within the leadership team. In a mature business model, ownership is often separated from management with most shares or financial interest sitting outside of the leadership team. The board of directors in this model needs to ensure that the professional management running the day-to-day business is doing so effectively, complying with legislation and returning the profits expected from investments made.

The MD's role in this size of organisation is more strategic, as there should be other managers in place to deliver sales, ensure quality products or services, service-customer enquiries and deliver work to external stakeholders. The role requires a leader who can think across all disciplines, integrate good ideas and build a successful organisation in a three-to-five-year timeframe. This leader is accountable for the ongoing design of the organisation to reflect changes in the external environment and optimise internal strengths.

One of the key characteristics of this model is that there is enough work in the organisation to form service elements. Service elements exist to support value-creation elements in the organisation and they are often grouped into functions. The quantity of service, the economies of scale and the specialisation of the services will impact whether they are separate elements in the organisation design rather than part of the value-chain elements. These service elements will report through to one of the members of the leadership team, depending on their function.

The service departments are normally cost-recovery operations but some may be allowed to contract out free capacity for income. Many service elements are expansions of the functional services found in the basic business model but the organisation may now be large enough for more specialist service departments such as the following:
- Training centres
- R&D centres
- Projects
- Facilities management
- Administration
- Information technology services
- Call centres
- Internal auditing

This mature business model with functional departments is termed a functional design model. It is probably the most widely applied in business and the most common design for this model. It relies on a centralised management function with a multidisciplined perspective on the business, supported by single-function departments. These departments specialise in their individual fields, such as production, sales, distribution, human resources and finance, and together they deliver the value chain for the organisation.

As long as the organisation is not too complex, it is an efficient design as there is specialisation and clarity of functions. This leads to clear definitions of functional roles and ease of training due to routine work. Management is centralised and so information tends to flow up the functional hierarchy for control and decision-making.

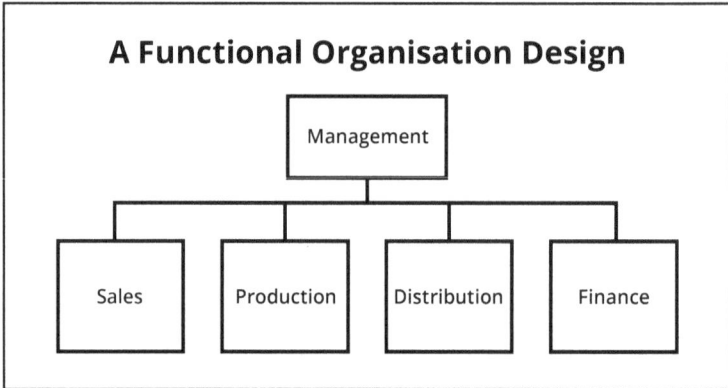

A Functional Organisation Design

```
                    ┌──────────────┐
                    │  Management  │
                    └──────┬───────┘
         ┌───────────┬─────┴──────┬────────────┐
   ┌─────┴─────┐┌────┴─────┐┌─────┴──────┐┌─────┴─────┐
   │   Sales   ││Production││Distribution││  Finance  │
   └───────────┘└──────────┘└────────────┘└───────────┘
```

Organisations utilising this model are likely to have competitors who provide customers with similar products and services, therefore efficient and effective delivery of these products become important factors, in addition to the quantity of sales. A competitive design of the organisation can lead to increased effectiveness of the value chain, creating higher margins and increased market share.

An organisation with this complexity can move work in and out of the organisation, open new locations, split work up into new departments, change technology and try to apply a range of best practices to improve performance.

Some of the design options open to this size of organisation to make it more effective are:

Outsourcing activities: The focus of the previous two models of organisation has been the growth of internal services to support the delivery of work to a growing number of stakeholders. As the business grows to this level of complexity, it may decide that some of its work can be done more effectively by an outsourced third party that focuses on this work as its core business. Service elements are most frequently the focus of outsourcing as many organisations find they cannot supply these services internally as effectively as a supplying organisation whose core focus is the provision of these specialist services. Some common types of outsourcing are distribution, computer maintenance and recruitment.

Geographical location: It is likely that this size of organisation will have customers in many locations and some may also have their value-chain processes in different places. This choice of whether to centralise or decentralise work will be critical to the performance of the business. A single location for activities can reduce costs through increasing productivity from economies of scale but multiple locations, such as placing sales teams close to the customer, can create the local loyalty of a start-up organisation.

Number of revenue-generating units: Having too much variety of work in a revenue centre can lead to poor performance. This variety could be in the form of manufacturing processes or customer specifications but it can also be due to the product's life cycle. Products at different stages of their life cycle require different approaches – from being a new product through to growth, maturity and decline. A new product may need a start-up style of environment to support its entrepreneurial growth, whereas a more mature product requires a more formal design. Dividing products and services into different income centres allows the work to be structured for each product's needs but this can also lead to duplicated costs.

81

Technology innovation and investment: Technology can radically change the design needed for an organisation. The digital market, for example, has transformed the design of businesses selling music and books. An internet sales distribution model supplying either physical products or downloaded products has led to the demise of the traditional design of many local book and record shops. Technology changes are likely to impact the most traditional designs: from banks introducing mobile banking to manufacturers using 3D printers. An organisation with an innovative organisation design optimising technology can take massive market shares from more traditional organisations.

Working patterns: These can change in any model but with more employees the options increase. Time-based designs are examples normally found within this model. The most common example is a shift-based design where work continues for longer than a normal eight-hour day. Another time-based design could be found in the agricultural sector, where the organisation changes depending on the season, ie substantially more employees would be needed during harvesting than during other seasons.

DESIGN MODELS FOR LINKING TEAM ROLES TOGETHER

As a business grows and moves toward business unit maturity, the number of employees increases and the organisation needs to decide how to structure teams within its value-chain process. The most traditional approach is to form teams within functions, so, for example, the finance team is split into accounting, costing and purchasing sub-teams, while a production function splits into raw material, manufacture and warehouse sub-teams. This functional model is the first of three main models in which to structure teams:

1. Functional structure: In this structure the employees reporting to a supervisor or manager all come from the same discipline/ function. This model is probably the most widely applied in this business model. It is an efficient structure as there is specialisation and clarity of functions. However, it is slow to respond to change and struggles to handle diversity of work.

This functional approach has limitations and some organisations choose to structure teams of mixed functional expertise into more outcomes-based results, such as the delivery of a product, a customer service or a project. In these teams, production, sales, finance and human resources will all work for a team leader in a process to deliver a valuable service or product.

2. Process structure: In this structure employees from more than one function or discipline are combined into teams to achieve the outputs of a department or work section. It can be viewed as the main alternative to the functional structure. The approach integrates functional expertise into multidisciplinary teams that are required to support the delivery of process value rather than purely functional outputs. It breaks down the functional silos, enables more effective output measurement and, from an organisational perspective, enables experience in managing multidisciplined teams from a broader range of management positions. However, it could lead to duplication of work compared with a functional structure.

There is a choice of the focus of each process team, which can be based on product/service, technology, geography or customer grouping

In this process approach, there will still be some functional roles supporting the overall management of the business unit or providing services to all teams. A normal rule of thumb in a process structure is that if a person spends the vast majority of their time working for a particular process, they should be part of the process team; if it is a non-regular service, then the role should be centralised.

Even when working in a process team, a functional team member, for example from finance, will have to follow the organisation and professional rules set by the finance function and will probably have a career path within the financial rather than process structure. This leads to many people working in a matrix structure, having two managers, one being functional and one for the delivery of an outcome.

3. Matrix structure: This approach involves the members of a team conducting work for two managers: one to direct day-to-day activities and the other from their functional speciality to direct the role on professional standards and approaches. This approach is frequently found in project work or more complex management positions. However, it is not an easy structure to maintain. It increases complexity to process management as it splits responsibility and accountabilities. This leads to a lack of clear focus on work deliverables.

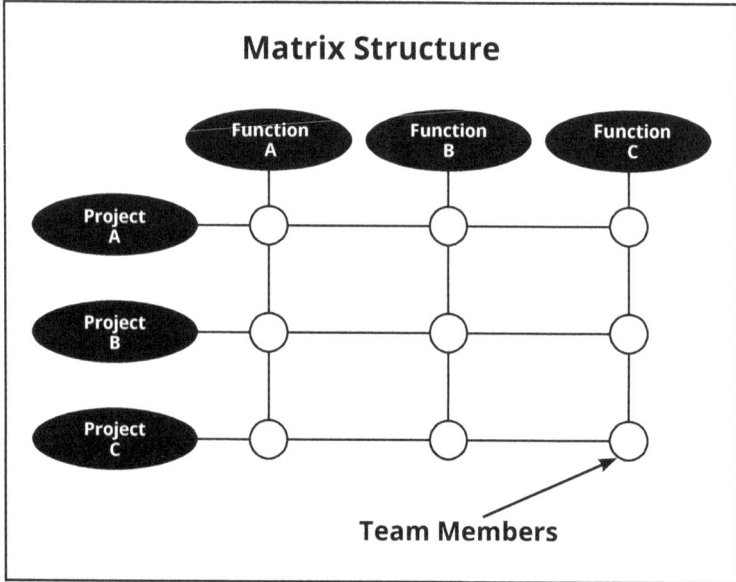

Matrix Structure

In large organisations there will be a combination of these three designs for teams in different departments. Dedicated professional departments such as financial accounts will be functional. Process structures are becoming more common with more multidisciplined teams seen as an effective approach, especially for manufacturing. A matrix approach can be very beneficial to organisations when they need project management or research and development.

The typical competitive edge of the mature business design organisation is through exhibiting better management practices in its chosen market than its competitors. These management practices are required because the organisation will have more stakeholders groups, some with up to 100 separate groups requiring more management of internal and external stakeholders.

The typical timeframe for measuring the performance of this size of organisation will be between one and two years, with annual business plans and results becoming important processes for management. From a financing point of view, the funds required will be large and most likely bank-sourced. The criteria for funding will be based on the organisation's ability to afford the loan and the quantity of organisational assets that can be used for security.

Even with all the design options for teams in this model, the underlying basis of this design is a functional one with profit accountability resting with the MD, who has to work across all functions supported by leaders from each core function/discipline in the management team. The corporate model allows the management of multiple businesses with profit accountability.

TRANSITIONING FROM A MATURE BUSINESS MODEL TO A CORPORATE MODEL

In a single business unit all decisions impacting profitability tend to require a decision from the leadership team and especially the MD. As the organisation becomes larger and more complex, the ability of the leadership team to not only direct current operations but also to set strategies for the future becomes strained. A major reason why the next model, the corporate model, is adopted is to enable leadership to cope with the size and complexity of the business unit in a manner that will support its continued growth.

This functional model reaches its limitations as the organisation grows and reaches its peak at around 1 000 employees. (The number of employees may not be an accurate measure of complexity – a large but stable organisation may have the same complexity as a small organisation undergoing radical strategic change.) As the organisation becomes larger and more complex in this design, it may become slow to respond to new stakeholder demands. The MD role is the only formal role accountable for profitability within the whole organisation, and there is a limit to the amount of complexity this role can manage.

Functional designs often face the challenge of barriers forming between the functions so that information is forced to go up the hierarchy rather than across to the function that needs it. This can lead to inefficiencies and internal competition for resources as the functions compete for political power in the organisation. A problem with centralised decision-making is that it can lead to a slow response to change and may struggle to handle a diversity of work.

The way to relieve this pressure is to create more business units that can be headed by their own profit-driven MD and leadership teams, allowing operational leadership to be pushed down to these teams and the original leadership team to focus on longer-term strategies and synergies across the business units. This transition from one business unit to multiple business units, which I have termed the corporate model, is a significant transition for the organisation and its leadership.

The key to this change is placing the right leaders in each business unit and focusing the roles in the central corporate function to create strategic value.

A business approach that could be seen to sit in between a mature business model and a corporate model is the franchise.

Many large organisations choose to mimic small businesses with local shops but support them with services that provide them with economies of scale. In a large organisation all the shops and employees are owned by the organisation and each is a revenue centre for the larger organisation. Examples of this type of business are retail chains such as Marks and Spencer or Greggs bakeries in the UK. To grow this approach requires a large investment by the organisation. This need for investment by the central organisation, which often slows growth into new markets, is partially overcome by a franchise approach.

A franchise approach has been hugely successful for some organisations and especially fast-food retailers. McDonald's, which was established in 1955, has over 32 000 franchise units. Other competitors have followed a similar approach with KFC having 16 000 units and Burger King 12 000 units. The organisation with the largest number of franchise units is 7-Eleven that began franchising in the mid-1960s and now has over 40 000 units.

In a franchise model, the outlet (or products/services) is owned by different organisations to the owner of the franchise brand. A franchise business is an organisation with a proven product and business approach and has chosen to sell copies of the approach to people who want to provide the same service or products in different locations. It is often a good way to expand quickly and attract capital into a business idea. However, it can be a restrictive approach for the franchisees who must conform to the rules and regulations of the parent company in terms of product scope, image, pricing and how to operate the business.

The franchise approach is attractive because it allows some of the benefits of being a larger organisation to be achieved through owning small businesses linked to the overall franchise. Each business in the franchise is in itself a viable business based on start-up or basic management models. The benefits of being part of a franchise include being part of a proven business idea, economies of scale for supplies, low spend to create the brand and access to support from the brand owner.

A franchise organisation works through standardising the approach and it reduces the number of stakeholders a franchisee has compared with a similar stand-alone organisation as shown here:

Stand-alone		Franchise	
Suppliers	5	Suppliers	3
Customers	3	Customers	3
Employees	1	Employees	1
Legal	3	Legal	3
Financial	3	Financial	2
Societal	2	Societal	1
Total	17	Total	13

A downside to the franchise approach is that the number of stakeholders for the whole franchise enterprise could be more than one large organisation producing the same volume of output as each franchisee creates its own stakeholders.

MODEL 4: CORPORATE

The forth model is the most exciting one for organisation design. It is the first model with multiple business units, and having more business units allows a whole range of new design options, many of which have the potential to deliver a competitive advantage.

In the corporate model there are two levels of profit accountability, with leadership teams in the business units each accountable for the profitability of their unit, and a more senior leadership team in the centre accountable for the sum of the profitability of all the business units. It is termed a corporate model due to the large scale of its operations.

This design has a new element: a head office/central function positioned above the business units, which focuses on overall profitability, and provides value through developing strategies and delivering synergies across the business units, rather than managing the operational performance within each business unit. As well as optimising the overall internal performance of the organisation, the central function manages many of the more external strategic issues on behalf of the business units. Sourcing finance for the group of businesses, presenting the external image, and investigating merger and acquisition opportunities are also all key activities in the central function.

The organisations applying this model are complex (it is used in some of the largest organisations in the world). There will be more interest in the work done, raising the number of separate stakeholder groups to more than 100. The major change is the increased number of external stakeholders. The organisations requiring this complexity of model will produce large amounts of varied work and will normally have between 500 and 10 000 employees. Due to the size of these organisations, there will generally be fewer national competitor organisations in the chosen market, with international competition being more prevalent.

The organisations would have chosen a part of a single industry or market in which to produce outputs, for example, in a mining organisation or a bank. The organisations are large and their size provides medium-term stability, with the timeframe for assessing and changing performance being within a five-year period. Both factors make these organisations attractive for funding through capital and bonds raised through stock markets.

This type of organisation's competitive edge lies in its ability to match the market requirements through the effective coordination of outputs of several multidisciplined management teams. However, these organisations are vulnerable to markets changing unexpectedly; an example of this is when the organisation focuses too much on local stakeholders and international competition enters their market taking a substantial market share.

For a business there is a cost involved to moving to the corporate model. The central structure will be expensive to resource and economies of scale will be diluted as a multidisciplined management team is needed in each unit. Each unit will also need to implement its own processes and systems to optimise profits. Part of the role of the central head office will be to define the extent of this scope for individuality in each business unit to optimise overall profitability.

Some of the reasons that an organisation may want to move from a mature business unit model to a multiple business unit model include:

Scope of leadership: As an organisation grows, it becomes more difficult for a single leadership team to manage all the activities that drive profitability. This growth will lead to more stakeholders via more locations, a wider variety of processes, more value chains and more interest in the organisation from external stakeholders. Leadership may also become stretched as it attempts to develop growth by, for example, trying to start up new ventures within a more mature organisation. Start-ups need focused leadership attention to grow, and can be constrained by the culture of a mature business. Splitting the organisation into more than one business unit increases the leadership structure, spreading out the work as well as pushing down the accountability for profitability management to the business unit teams, thus leaving the central team to focus on strategy delivery and change. The extra cost of management structures ought to be offset by the growth generated from implementing these strategies.

Growth into a new market: To grow into a new market, particularly if it is remote from the main organisation, often requires that it operates as a separate business unit that can make the decisions it needs to make in rapid response to its specific market and stakeholder needs.

A need for clarity as to where profit is made in the organisation: Often when a business unit becomes too large, the income and costs are consolidated into profit at too high a level to fully understand the whole organisation's performance. Separating a business into more business units is an effective way to identify which parts of the organisation are creating profits or losses.

Different stages of a product life cycle: To a certain extent, one would expect some alignment between business life-cycle models and the models for design of an organisation. The Boston Consulting Group's life-cycle matrix model is a good example of a model that can be linked to the organisation models as illustrated below:
- A **Question Mark** business would have simple models, such as a start-up or basic management.
- A **Star** business would be moving through the least complex models quickly to probably become a mature business model.
- A **Cash Cow** would either have a mature business unit model or corporate design model.
- A **Dog** could be either a small business that has not yet grown to a star or is in the process of downsizing from a Cash Cow business.

When an organisation has multiple products or markets at different stages in the life cycle, it can be beneficial to separate some out to different business units to give them the leadership focus they require for their particular life-cycle stage.

Industry regulation or legislation: There can be legal or regulatory reasons why different parts of an organisation have to be managed separately. A grey area between this corporate model and the next global model is where small business units have different shareholding or ownership rights but only one board for the organisation.

Technology/business activity: This approach would be to consolidate similar processes and technologies into specialised business units, rather than to duplicate these processes within each business unit. This specialisation could lead to economies of scale that allow the whole organisation to become more competitive. These groupings will each want different work from the organisation. If the work is different in each unit, it will generally mean that a specialised approach to managing this work will be effective if the business unit's technology activities are large enough.

Customers have different needs: As organisations become larger, customer stakeholders can usually be defined into more precise groupings. This could mean that the type of work needs to be managed differently. If the groupings contain enough customers, then separate business units may be the best way to deliver this work.

Brand: The creation of different brands can either be at a product level or by the creation of a whole new business unit that may compete directly with other brands in the same organisation. The separation of a brand into a stand-alone business unit makes it easier to assess the value of that brand.

Different geographical locations: Location is probable the most common reason for separating a part of an organisation into a separate business unit. The distance does not necessarily have to be a substantial one – it could be a shop or restaurant operating in the same town, but managed as separate business units or profit centres. Larger business units are normally segregated regionally or nationally.

Language: If an organisation decides to locate to a country with a language different to the one used in the majority of its business, it may make sense to manage that part of the business separately as its systems and controls will have to be in that language. However, using multiple languages in an organisation increases its complexity and costs, so some larger organisations choose a single language for their business.

Currencies: Similar to the language factor, differing currencies usually mean that systems and controls have to be implemented that are different to the rest of the organisation.

A preparation for divestment: If a part of an organisation is being prepared for sale, then separating it into a stand-alone business unit enables an assessment of its profitability. To sell off part of a business that is not a business unit requires the implementation of systems, processes and structures to create a business unit that is a viable business. In the UK The Royal Bank of Scotland and Lloyds Bank were faced with this challenge when the European Union directed that they must sell several hundred branches and their customer bases to competitors as a result of receiving government support.

Mergers and acquisitions: Sometimes a business unit model is a temporary one, for example directly after an acquisition when two businesses may still be operating separately until they are fully merged. When organisations merge or are acquired, they create a new organisation. This larger organisation will require design changes in the dominant organisation. Sometimes the growth resulting from this change leads to the new organisation moving to the next band of complexity. If two mature businesses model organisations merge, the most appropriate designs for them would be either a larger mature business or a corporate business. Acquisitions are normally initiated by a mature business unit or a more complex design model organisation because they have the resources to manage a merger while maintaining an ongoing business. In a merger, the least complex scenario will be when the culture and work complexity of each organisation is similar. If one of these factors is different, it will increase the complexity of the merger, and if both are different, the merger will be highly complex.

WORK COMPLEXITY AND ALLOCATING WORK IN A CORPORATE MODEL

From an organisation design perspective, reaching this model offers an organisation the opportunity to strategically leverage the design of its business. In moving from one business unit, delivering the chosen value chain(s) to stakeholders, to multiple business units, there is a new opportunity to define the focus of each of the units differently to create a strategic competitive advantage. This competitive advantage could be achieved by splitting the units into different parts of the value chain, or by dividing them into geographical regions or customer groupings. In this model of design, the design itself is a strategic decision. Leaders of this model of organisation need to understand that their choice of unit definition will bring for each option its own pros and cons to the whole organisation.

In a corporate model, the size and complexity of each business unit will vary depending on its history, life cycle and market potential. The complexity of the business unit will require it to be modelled either as a start-up, a basic management or a mature model. Within a larger organisation a new business unit could be initiated as a start-up model especially if entering a new market. This small team would grow an idea to test its feasibility before more resources are invested. Other business units are likely to be at different stages of maturity, with some even in decline. This model addresses the needs of these different units to have their own management and business focus, which matches their maturity, customer base and internal processes.

To gain synergies there is normally a centralisation of some services for all the business units, which provides an economy of scale benefit. Because these activities exist to support the business units they have a different role to the more strategic central functions. This differentiation often obscures the size of some head offices when centralised service for the units and strategic services are located in the same head office.

Organisations that have grown successfully from a start-up to a mature business model have needed to be reasonably good at identifying the work the organisation has to do and who in the organisation should do it. The move to a corporate model requires a whole new level of complexity of organisation design, and it is the model where the impact of not getting it right can lead to the failure of the business.

The division of work in a corporate model entails two key changes to a single business unit. Firstly, there are many more options of where to place work in the organisation, and, secondly, the timeframe of work for this complexity of organisation is normally a major step up from a single business unit.

The strategies and policies that are the main focus of work in the corporate centre should direct the future of the organisation for a five-year timeframe at least, but their impact could be much longer. This is a new level of work complexity that most smaller business units do not require on a full-time basis; instead they may develop a three-to-five-year plan that they review once a year.

The options of where work can be placed in a corporate model expand due to the following design characteristics in this model:
- The **corporate centre,** which is unique to this design.
- **Multiple business units,** which provide an opportunity to redesign how these business units are structured, and a

choice of which parts of the value chain the organisation should focus its efforts on.

- **Dedicated service units** and a choice of where to place services in the design: in the business unit, in a service unit, in a division/region, in the corporate centre or no longer in the organisation but rather outsourced.
- Options to group business units into **divisions or regions** each with their own central structures leading to more options for how to group business units and services.
- The choice of **geographical location** for each element in the design.
- The **grouping of units** in a single location or widely spread out in multiple locations.

These characteristics lead to a wide variety of design options for this model.

The volume of work the organisation chooses to do will also be key to its design and differentiate it from competitors. Organisations of this size can be market leaders choosing to invest in innovations smaller organisations cannot afford. Their choices will impact costs – the right ones will deliver returns from the investment, while the wrong ones will result in the organisation becoming less competitive. Examples of where large organisations could invest in are research and development or expanding into new markets, both of which may take several years to prove their viability but would provide a head start on more cautious competitors.

The challenge in this model is to define the business units as these are the centres of profitability of the organisation and therefore key to its success.

THE DESIGN OF THE BUSINESS UNIT ELEMENTS IN THE CORPORATE MODEL

In the more complex design models of an organisation, the choices of organisation work design become more varied and can become critical in the strategic competitiveness of the organisation.

Defining the business unit(s) is the starting point of corporate model organisation design as it positions where profit or value-creation work takes place in the organisation.

A business unit is the centre of value creation for a business organisation. In terms of this discussion a business unit is defined as the point of profit-generation and management. In non-business organisations, measurements of service delivery to costs would be applied to assess value creation rather than profit. Profit is an important concept in work design because its management dictates that the following takes place:

- A multidisciplined view of the organisation so that work for the stakeholders in the organisation is achieved.
- Profit is created via the interaction of all functions – both revenue- and cost-focused.
- Leadership has to have a general management ability to manage across all functions.
- An ability to invest in change to increase revenue and decrease costs.
- To sustain profitability the impact of short- and long-term plans has to be taken into account.
- If a part of an organisation is set up as a profit centre, it should be possible to operate this business as an independent organisation if it were to break away from the larger organisation.

If the leadership of a profit-orientated business unit is to be held accountable, it must have the authority to make the necessary decisions to improve profitability. These decisions would include the ability to plan and control work, set policies and procedures relating to the unit, manage revenues and costs/resources and satisfy stakeholders. These will probably be conducted under the umbrella of the larger organisation's defined scope for the business unit and its policies, systems, rules and regulations. These rules impact the business unit's freedom to operate and make decisions.

Regarding size, a business unit could encompass the whole organisation or consist of two or three employees. Larger organisations will tend to have multiple business units. If centralised control is required, there will tend to be larger business units, however, with more decentralisation, smaller business units will normally be found.

In an organisation the other management and service elements only exist because of these value-creation elements. Above the business units will be a direction and coordination function, normally in the form of a head office, and linked to this will be corporate staff who provide strategic services for all the business units. Within each business units there will be departments and normally centralised staff providing services to all departments.

ORGANISATION WORK DESIGN OPTIONS IN RESPECT TO THE SPLIT AND FOCUS OF BUSINESS UNITS IN THE CORPORATE MODEL

The challenge in choosing the best business-unit mix is knowing which one is most suited to support the organisation's strategy, and when to change the current model to a more competitive one.

The needs of stakeholders and the chosen work processes in the organisation play a large role in defining the focus of a business unit. Redefining the focus of value-adding work can have a major impact on the performance of an organisation, such as a move from a technology focus to a customer focus for a business unit.

The business unit models that are options for the work design of value-creation elements in an organisation are listed as follows with their individual pros and cons.

CORE DESIGN MODELS

These models are the main core choices of how leadership can view their organisation though the design of business units. These designs reflect the most important processes that deliver value for the organisation and hopefully the item(s) the customers want to buy.

Business units in a corporate model follow a process design approach, which splits up functions into multidisciplinary teams that are required to support the delivery of process value rather than purely functional outputs. The work allocated to a business unit will be a process delivered by a multidisciplined team. In a corporate model, the three choices for splitting up work into processes are by technology, products or customer groupings.

TECHNOLOGY DESIGN MODEL

This model is appropriate when the resources for each type of technology are different and/or the processes used are specialised. In this model the customer wants the output from a technology-based process, often raw materials or the processing of raw materials. Mining and petrochemical companies are good examples. A mine will apply a technology approach when there is an ore body to mine. Each mine will apply the same or similar technologies to mine the ore body. In a large organisation there may be several different types of technologies that have different needs but can be grouped together in business units. A mining company may choose to group underground mining separately from opencast mining. A petrochemical organisation may split oil exploration, rig operations and refining into three different technology business units.

In these organisation designs, the challenge is to manage the technical approach successfully. The output is likely to be similar if not identical to competitors so the effective use of technology provides a competitive advantage.

The role of the central structure is to keep up to date with technology, provide market-leading expertise to optimise technology, identify where to apply the technology, manage the risks in applying the technology, find customers for the outputs, and ensure synergy across the business units applying different technologies within the same value chain.

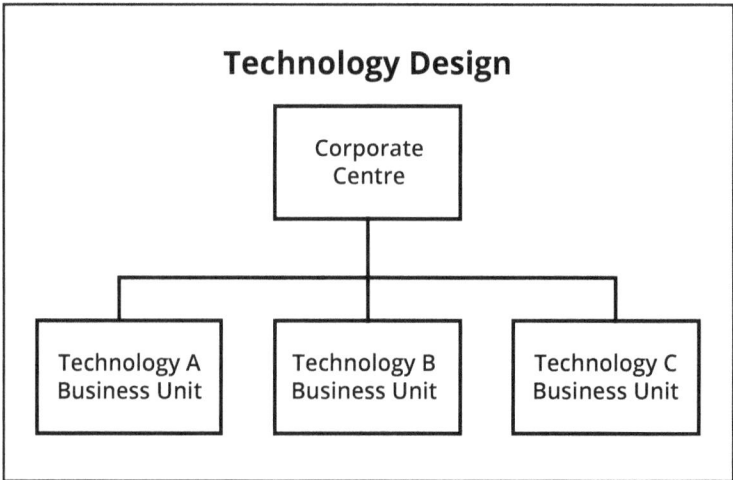

Technology Design

```
                    ┌─────────────┐
                    │  Corporate  │
                    │   Centre    │
                    └──────┬──────┘
          ┌────────────────┼────────────────┐
   ┌──────┴──────┐  ┌──────┴──────┐  ┌──────┴──────┐
   │ Technology A│  │ Technology B│  │ Technology C│
   │Business Unit│  │Business Unit│  │Business Unit│
   └─────────────┘  └─────────────┘  └─────────────┘
```

If the final product or service to the customer has to pass through more than one of these technology business units, then the value chain needs to be effectively managed to ensure coordination within the whole organisation. A wide variation in the skills and profile of employees within the different technologies could create different cultures within the organisation that might be difficult to manage.

PRODUCT/SERVICE DESIGN MODEL

In this model the customer wants an output, ie a specific product or service. The organisation will have multiple processes in place to make or deliver that output, be it a washing machine or car. The manufacturing processes may be complex but it is unlikely that the customer is interested, their focus being on the finished product.

Each business unit could build the same product, a different product or a small range of products. It is a structure that allows a popular product to be sold in a range of markets. The business units are defined by product, service or group. This is a very common structure and assumes that if the products are made for the right price, customers will want to buy them. The business units will be focused on sales volumes and their relative share of that product's market. In the example on page 118, the organisation is split up by product teams, which normally have functional or process structures within them. This model allows a dedicated focus on each product and its development, however, it can also lead to duplication of work and confusion for customers requiring a range of products.

In this model the product is the focus. There is an assumption that if products are made, customers will want to buy them. This allows the organisation to focus on producing high-quality products or services with a large degree of repetitiveness allowing for highly efficient processes. This specialisation often leads to product leadership and the development of market-leading products.

Product Design

```
                    Corporate
                     Centre
          ┌─────────────┼─────────────┐
     Product A      Product B      Product C
```

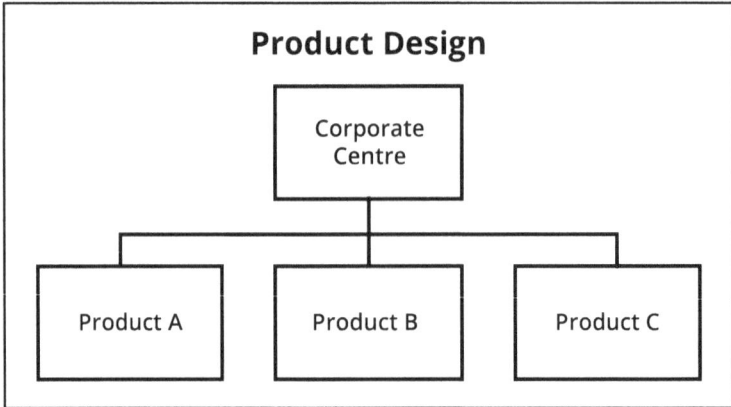

To a certain extent globalisation has taken this approach to a new level where huge production facilities can manufacture all the products needed for regional or world markets and many localised manufacturing operations find they cannot compete with these economies of scale.

The process can lose efficiency when customers want different products or a mixture of products from different business units.

CUSTOMER SEGMENTATION DESIGN MODEL

This approach is similar to the product and technology models in that the business units are differentiated by the most important aspect of the organisation. In this case it's different types of customers. Customer-centric design models are popular as companies recognise that loyal customers are often the most profitable. A customer-centric organisation would normally have business units according to customer segments (a customer segment is a group of customers with the same characteristics such as age-group, product preference or spending appetite) where the profitability of that segment is measured and managed. This approach would be applicable if an organisation's customer base is easily segmented and each segment has different needs. The model allows for good customer focus and the measurement of customer performance. As with the other model options, the approach could lead to a duplication of work.

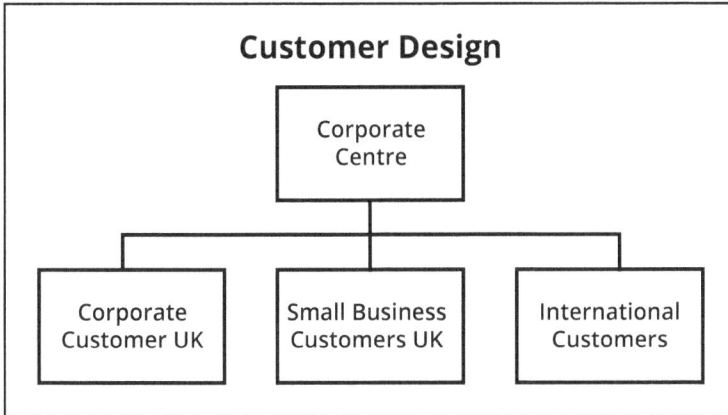

```
┌─────────────────────────────────────────────────────┐
│                  Customer Design                      │
│              ┌───────────────────┐                    │
│              │     Corporate      │                   │
│              │      Centre        │                   │
│              └───────────────────┘                    │
│   ┌──────────────┐ ┌──────────────┐ ┌──────────────┐  │
│   │  Corporate    │ │Small Business│ │ International │  │
│   │ Customer UK   │ │ Customers UK │ │  Customers    │  │
│   └──────────────┘ └──────────────┘ └──────────────┘  │
└─────────────────────────────────────────────────────┘
```

These three business-unit designs are the most common but there are further options that may be suitable depending on the work in an organisation.

103

MORE COMPLEX DESIGN MODELS

PROJECT DESIGN MODEL

Many manufacturing and service organisations create a solution unique to a client's needs through the delivery of a project. This is a common organisation design model in, for example, many large construction companies, consultancies and project-orientated divisions of larger organisations, such as R&D or IT departments. Each project would become a profit-orientated business unit until its solution is delivered. The individuals within the unit are frequently managed in a matrix structure. The approach focuses on individual projects and there is an expectation that when one project is completed, another will start.

In a corporate model design following this approach, there would be a strategic corporate centre as well as multiple project centres – normally separated geographically – each controlling a number of projects.

In this type of organisation design, the project centre functions are generally stable but the delivery business units can vary dramatically, in size, number and complexity, depending on the quantity and stage of work. Functions include selling, resourcing and funding the projects. It is important that the centre provides the continuity of approach, such as standards, policies and culture, so that clients can be reassured that each project will meet its promised standard.

The project team will have clarity on the work that needs to be achieved and be familiar with all the client's requirements.

This model allows the duplication of a good service into new markets but with a focus on the local delivery of the service a region requires. It is closely aligned to delivering a specific customer need but the resources have to be highly flexible because once the project is completed, they will be reallocated; and contracts ended until more work is won. Good examples of this model can be found in business or IT consultancies that open offices in different countries or regions to service local projects.

A key role of the corporate centre in this model is to ensure quality and internal cultural standards across all regions as this is the basis of the organisation's brand. The organisation needs to decide what factors are similar in all centres and how much variation is allowed for local conditions.

Too much or too little work puts a strain on this model as the stable centre is frequently too high a cost if there is too little work in the project business units. If there is too much work the competencies in the centre will become stretched and the quality of work could fall below the desired level.

Volume of work fluctutations can inhibit the growth of these organisations. A successful corporate centre will position the organisation for growth, expanding in growth regions and reallocating resources from regions in decline.

Project Design

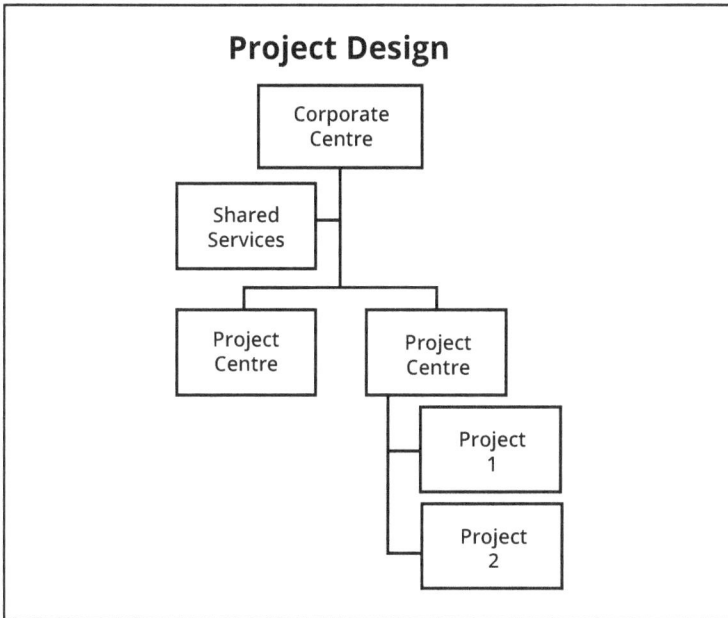

GEOGRAPHIC DESIGN MODEL

This model is very common in corporate organisations. It is a common design for mature business units with regards to their location of income and cost centres, and the underlying design for the global model. The business units are split by their location, which is generally per region, but increasingly common by country. A location split brings the organisation close to its customer base or its resource inputs, thereby creating a local organisation. It is especially applicable when transport costs are high or the delivery of services is necessary at customer sites.

The centre in this model has to manage customer solutions covering several regions and to ensure that competition between regions is not destructive. This model is normally linked to one of the core models of customer, product or technology.

This approach can result in a duplication of services in each location leading to a loss of economies of scale. It also requires a clear differentiation of the customer service so that customers can purchase what they need from each location.

CHANNEL ORGANISATION MODEL

This design can be seen as a form of customer segmentation. By defining how customers buy rather than examining their demographics, this model focuses on the links between products and customers via their purchasing channels.

Types of channels include retail shops, wholesale warehouses, call centres, the internet and, more recently, digital mobile formats. The differences between channels are becoming greater and the approaches used in each channel may vary.

Each channel is likely to have features that are attractive to customers, for example, convenience, but for the organisation different cost structures would need to be established for each channel. Optimising costs by attracting more customers to a low-cost channel could make a significant difference to an organisation. These costs are likely to be based on the infrastructure and process required to service the channels. If costs vary significantly between the channels this could be another reason why a channel business unit design is appropriate for the organisation.

For most organisations, information about how and where their customers buy is vital, and with new technologies transforming many markets, understanding how customer buying patterns are changing could be important for an organisation's success. If this is a key strategic challenge for the organisation, structuring it by channel could be the best way to monitor this transformation and ensure that the organisation's processes are aligned to the needs of each channel.

The profitability of each channel can be managed in this approach but it can make it more difficult to monitor overall product or customer profitability. It requires effective customer-relationship management information to keep track of customers across several business units.

In this model, the role of the centre is to manage product and customer information and to ensure that the competitiveness between the business unit channels is positive and aligned to strategy. If a bank wants to migrate some customers from branches to its internet channel to reduce costs, it would be counterproductive for the branch unit to invest to retain customers in its branches.

The challenge for the organisation is to define how much overlap there is between channels. Customers may choose the internet to buy simple products but prefer face-to-face contact for more complex purchases. Customers also may look at the physical product in one channel, ie a shop, but choose to buy it later via another channel, ie online. If there is significant overlap between channels or customers using several channels to complete a purchase, this model may not be suitable

LIFE-CYCLE DESIGN MODEL

The requirements of an organisation are different depending on where they are in their life cycle. Entrepreneurial organisations need to invest in all their resources but especially in allowing their leadership time to nurture and grow their idea. (Some organisations do this through idea-incubator units and research laboratories.) As the organisation moves through the growth phase to maturity and eventually into decline, the needs of the business units change, for example the investment and profitability profiles are different in each stage of the life cycle.

Some corporate designs may be in growth, maturity or decline depending on their chosen markets, however, most corporate designs should have business units in each phase of the life cycle with some growing as others decline or are sold. A model of design could be to split the business units by their stage in the life cycle. Another possible model could be to define business units in respect of their maturity in line with the life-cycle approach. This model is rarely applied in its purest sense as it is difficult to define organisations, and suggesting that part of an organisation is declining could lead to a self-fulfilling prophecy (when, instead what the organisation really needed was innovation). However, many organisations have in their portfolio a range of products at different stages of the life cycle and this approach recognises that the leadership and systems approaches for each of the stages in a life cycle are different.

Maturity of Business Design

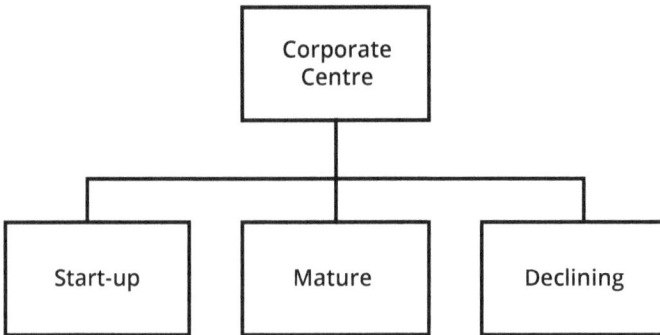

Corporate Centre

| Start-up | Mature | Declining |

In a large organisation there will be units of different sizes as well as at different stages of growth: some are start-up, others more mature, but each will need an appropriate strategy either to maintain their current performance or to grow to the next model. An organisation wanting to grow will ensure that the plans and strategies are appropriate for each complexity of business.

VIRTUAL CORPORATION

This design is becoming much more mainstream due to globalisation and technology. In his book *Designing Organizations*, Jay R. Galbraith, defines it as: "The virtual corporation, sometimes called the networked organization... is created by extensive contracting out of activities once performed in-house." (Page 135, Jossey-Bass, 2002)

The typical virtual corporation has a clearly defined business intent, and focuses on the core value-delivery parts of the business. These core activities will be ones where there is a competitive advantage and they are strategically important to maintain control. It is through these core activities that the business is driven, and all other activities required for value delivery to customers are outsourced. This means that an organisation may design and market a product but the manufacture, distribution and physical sale of the product is conducted by other organisations. The level of commitment from these other organisations to the main organisation will be a factor in the quantity of their business, which is dependent on the main organisation. An organisation that only has a small percentage of its business dependent on orders from the main organisation is likely to be less committed than one with a large percentage.

There are many benefits to the main organisation as it can focus on what it is good at; it can lower costs through international or best-price contracting; it has low levels of capital expenditure and overheads; and many costs will be matched to volumes of sales. The risks to a virtual corporation include contractors who may move to competitors; the escalation of costs when supplying unique services; and the challenges of managing a value chain across many different organisations, including trying to achieve common values such as standards for customer service and product quality.

More and more small businesses are enabled by virtual company approaches and few large organisations do not apply at least some virtual corporation approaches for their non-core activities.

MIXED ORGANISATION DESIGNS

A mixed organisation design is when the business units within an organisation are a mix of the design options listed above. In the example below, technology, customer and geographical models are applied. This approach recognises that the design needs of business units can be different but it is a design option that is more complex to manage and will require effective information systems at its centre to consolidate performance from each business unit into a combined picture of the organisation.

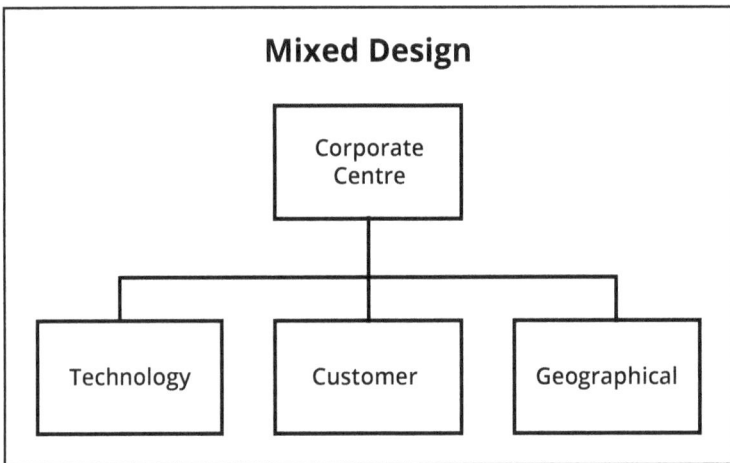

Mixed Design

Corporate Centre

Technology | Customer | Geographical

This approach is applied in many of the largest corporates and one of its most common mixed designs is the Front/Back Hybrid Structure described by Jay R. Galbraith in his book *Designing Organizations* as: "The Front/Back Hybrid Structure is a combination of product and market structures. It consists of a front-end structure that is focused on market segments or geography (or both) and a back-end structure that is focused on products and technologies. Both the front and the back ends are multi-functioned structures in themselves." (Page 116, Jossey-Bass, 2002)

The front-end units allow a customer focus to source and cross-sell all the products the sector of customers want from back-end product units whose dedicated focus on each product allows them to be effectively delivered.

This approach tends to have more business units than a simpler model. This makes it more complex, resulting in its having higher costs, being more difficult to manage and possibly leading to more competition within the business for scarce resources. Specialist resources used by both front and back units, such as marketing, are often centralised in the corporate centre to reduce duplicated costs.

The differing designs lead to complexity in organisation management but can also lead to a competitive advantage through a strategic focus that a simpler model would not provide.

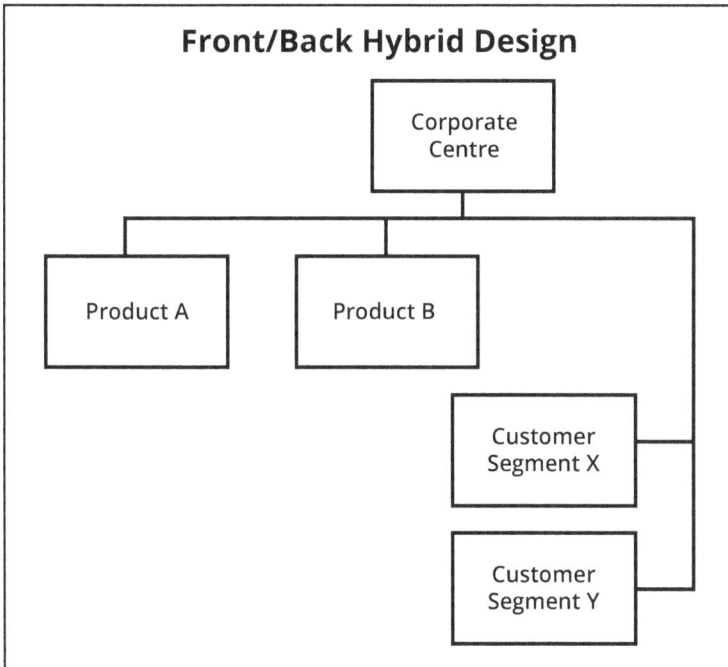

Front/Back Hybrid Design

Corporate Centre

Product A

Product B

Customer Segment X

Customer Segment Y

A mixed organisation design for a business unit is difficult to manage and requires excellent management information to create the pictures in each business unit. The largest organisations have the financial strength to implement highly complex information systems and a front-back hybrid model can aid competitiveness. It can be tempting for smaller organisations to try and design a business unit with several different profitability drivers, such as products, location or customer groupings, but this could lead to confusion and inefficiency.

It is normally much more efficient to choose one option for a business unit definition and support it with great information on other profit drivers in the business.

DESIGNING SERVICE ELEMENTS TO SUPPORT THE DELIVERY OF BUSINESS UNIT VALUE

The organisation design of services required by this size of organisation creates a huge variety of options. These options to deliver services to the business units have the potential to differentiate the organisation from its competitors. An organisation that can gain an advantage through its services ought to show benefits in one or more of the following performance measures:
- Cost
- Response time to change
- Speed of product development
- Quality
- Customer satisfaction

Services exist in every business unit. In the simplest unit they often make up just a portion of the employee's tasks. Most services will be supplied by functions within the business units or by teams in the management centres. In bigger organisations service elements can be much larger and can be designed as a large department or a separate service unit. Service elements exist to support the value-creation elements in the organisation.

When the business units have been defined, then the service elements can be designed. The quantity of service, the economies of scale and the specialisation of the services will impact whether they are regarded as separate elements in the organisation design rather than as part of the business unit or management elements. Service elements can range from a small team to a whole division made up of multiple service units. The larger service units will be managed by multidisciplined management teams and could employ thousands of staff.

Identifying business models that require less service elements can have a major impact on the competitiveness of an organisation. To achieve this, some organisations have 'off-shored' their services by moving services, such as call centres, to cheaper locations with India being particularly popular.

Where to position a service in a design depends on the cost of service provider, how often the service is required, the criticality of the service in terms of value creation and/or risk to the business, economies of scale and the speed of service delivery required. If the frequency of service provision is high or the speed of delivery to the business unit is high, then placing the service within the business unit is often the optimum approach. As a general rule of thumb, a service that is used day to day to support the delivery of the value chain should be placed within the business unit.

Services with high levels of criticality to business performance are normally retained by a business, while less critical services are considered for outsourcing. Service elements can either be placed as a cost centre within a business unit, or as a separate service unit, either in a divisional structure, a corporate centre or in a global centre. The general principle being that they should be positioned close to the work they support

Larger service groupings should produce more economies of scale that should mean that a bigger organisation should have a lower unit cost for services than a smaller one.

Services often rely heavily on technology and IT to deliver their services. Locating the service delivery close to the work can develop systems and processes directly aligned to that work that may outweigh economies-of-scale benefits.

The focus of service elements is normally functional because it is discipline-specific, however, some service elements are moving towards a process design. Other services are based around a technology such as a call centre infrastructure. In larger organisations there can be multiple service elements that are duplicated geographically to be close to business units.

Centralisation and decentralisation philosophies in an organisation are a key driver of the service design with a centralisation approach drawing services away from the business units to centre functions.

The design challenges for service elements are similar to business units. If they are small they are likely to be functionally structured as teams or departments. As they grow larger into service units, they will have large numbers of employees and assets requiring multifunctional management teams supported by multifunctional departments to lead and internally service the needs of the unit.

In a complex organisation there are a number of design options based around where services are placed: ie do they stay in the business units, service units, divisional structures, in the head office, or are they bought in from external suppliers?

For the services commonly found in business units the corporate model means there will be more of them and they are likely to be bigger. This leads to an opportunity to explore the consolidation of some services into larger units for economies of scale. These larger service units are specialist elements, normally functionally orientated but sometimes based on a process output. These units can employ thousands of employees supporting the overall value chain of the organisation.

In a corporate model there will also be a wider variety of services that are not economical for a single business unit to employ. The size of the organisation makes it feasible to employ full-time specialist services only required irregularly in most business units such as

- Tax advisors
- Corporate lawyers
- Public relations
- Strategists
- Remuneration managers
- Pension-fund experts
- IS developers
- Auditors

The service elements in this size of organisation are most frequently outsourced, as many organisations find they cannot supply these services as effectively internally as a supplying organisation whose core focus is the provision of these specialist services. This is partly due to the attractiveness of big contracts these larger organisations can negotiate with suppliers.

This model is often the leader in challenging market norms by offering the service in new ways led by innovation, which the organisation has enough financial strength to fund. An example of this could be international outsourcing where an organisation needs to be large enough so that the volume of benefits justifies the challenge of moving work to a new country.

In the corporate model the service design needs to reflect the environment of the business unit. In an environment with high levels of service competition, a supplier design – where many activities are outsourced – may be the most effective for the organisation as market forces should ensure the efficiency of suppliers. In a market with few potential suppliers, a design where services are supplied internally may be the most effective as the organisation can employ the resources it requires and manage its own level of service. This means that in different geographical locations the design of services can look very different even if the business units produce the same products.

In the process to stabilise the corporate design, there is frequently a period of oscillation between centralisation and decentralisation of control. It is difficult for leaders used to having hands-on control of an organisation in a mature business model to step back from operational management and focus on culture, synergy and strategy.

A centralisation approach to services can increase the perceived size of the head office. It can confuse the role of a head office by inflating its size through delivering operational services needed by the value chain as well as strategic services. If taken too far, the centralisation of services may restrict the business units from managing their profitability as they lose control of key services impacting profit management.

Large service units can become problematic in a corporate model. In large organisations service units can lose their connection with supporting the business unit value chain. They can start to become an empire in their own right and set policies dictating how the organisation should work for the ease of the service even if this is not aligned to customer needs. This dysfunctional approach will make the organisation as a whole less efficient.

In designing the organisation, it is important to remember that the service would not be required without the value chain. Being cheaper is not always best for the customer. Service delivery should be seen from the perspective of the part it plays in delivering the value chain and not in isolation as a cost.

The service provision is normally one of the largest cost areas of an organisation, and making the wrong design choices or not changing design as the market changes can have a major impact on competitiveness.

In order to manage and direct several business units, an effective corporate centre or head office is required

THE ROLE OF THE CENTRAL CORPORATE STRUCTURE/HEAD OFFICE

In the corporate model there is an assumption that there is a new level of work complexity required that is not found in a single business unit. This work at the most senior level of the organisation is focused on the long-term strategy of the integrated business unit organisation. In a corporate model the leadership of each business unit must manage the day-to-day running of its unit to achieve profitability and performance goals set by the central function. The central function therefore plays a more strategic role. As well as agreeing on performance targets for each unit, it will buy and sell business units, allocate scarce capital, create a synergistic culture across the units and reduce costs through limiting the number of stakeholders.

In organisations following one of the first three design models, elements of this work is taken on by leadership whose responsibilities include strategy and culture development and alignment with external stakeholders. In the corporate model, these functions are the focus of the whole centralised team.

This centralised team or corporate centre, which is a key element of the corporate design model, often resides in a head office separated from the leadership teams of the business units. In a single business unit there may also be centralised leadership but it is focused on the performance of that business unit.

Most corporate model head offices will accommodate the senior executives and their support functions required to support strategic executive decision-making. The corporate team produces value for the organisation by:
- Sourcing and allocating capital and funding.
- Creating a more effective organisation design than competitors, including legal and tax structures.
- Investment and divestment of business units.

- Setting the synergy rules for the organisation, which will also have a large impact on its culture.
- Creating the image and profile of the organisation to external stakeholders especially in terms of investors and regulators.
- Setting profit and performance expectations for individual business units, and appointing the most senior leaders of the business units to deliver them.
- Protecting the organisation from medium- and long-term risks.

The normal functions found within a corporate office to deliver this value are:

- Strategy formulation
- Company secretariat
- Financial accounting
- Legal and tax advisors
- Public relations
- Executive information management
- Staff policies and organisation design
- Enterprise risk

The corporate leaders will answer to the organisation's board, which will be the most senior accountable body of the organisation. The board will appoint the CEO and it is the approval body for the strategic proposals produced in the corporate functions. In this model the legal structure of the business units within it can be complex, and many organisations have boards to govern legally separate business or service units within the organisation

WHAT IS THE OPTIMUM SIZE OF A CORPORATE CENTRE?

There is regular scrutiny in the media from industry commentators regarding the size and cost of centralised management structures of organisations. A small structure is frequently seen as more desirable as it reflects the organisation as lean and cost-effective. However, studies such as the one cited below have had very little success in identifying the optimum size of a head office.

'The optimum size of a Head Office?' Ashridge Strategic Management Centre's analysis of 100 major UK companies found the following:
- The largest number of staff in a head office was 2 500.
- The smallest number of staff in a head office was 10.
- Thirteen companies with a total payroll size of between 10 000 and 50 000 people had head office sizes of 100 people or less.
- Five companies with a total payroll size of between 10 000 and 50 000 people had a head office size of more than 1 000 people.

Adapted from G. Foster, 'The Central Question', in *Management Today*, 1994.

The general result of this study was that there is no standard for the right size of a head office and whether its size is appropriate depends on how effectively it supports the value creation of the whole organisation.

A head office structure can be used in a mature business model as well as the corporate model. In a mature business model the head office manages the organisation's profitability from the sum of its income and cost centres. In the global business model (the next model up from corporate) a new head office is required above the corporate model. The differences in the models reflect one of the major challenges in defining and comparing head offices in the context of the business model being managed.

In a corporate model the separation between the corporate centre and shared services to support the business units is frequently unclear as they often share the same location. These shared services located with the central team can obscure the activities of the central corporate team and create the impression of a large head office. Some of the more common service functions located centrally or as service elements outside of the business units are:

- Internal auditing
- Research and development
- Marketing
- Project management
- Product/facility design
- Centralised education training and development
- Human resource advisors
- Financial advisors
- IT advisors
- Centralised administration

The picture becomes even more complex if the same location is also suitable for some of the business units and operational functions, such as call centres, manufacturing plants and administration centres, as it is difficult to differentiate between the operational structures and the centralised management structures.

When one organisation is compared with another, the size of their head offices can differ even if they have both been designed effectively. The main factors influencing the size of head offices are the following:

- The size and complexity of the organisation – whether the model is a business unit or a global organisation.
- The range and differentiation of the organisation's products and markets.
- The level of international activity in the organisation.
- The influence of a parent company and whether any services are sourced from it.
- The geographical location of the organisation.

- The quantity of strategic and capital expansion taking place or being planned.
- The quantity of required value-chain integration across the different units in the organisation.
- The organisation's approach to centralisation or decentralisation.
- The economic placement of scarce skills.
- The number of operational elements residing in the same location.

Sometimes the perception that a head office structure is too large is inaccurate and it is efficient in supporting value creation in the organisation; however, frequently the perception is appropriate and the structures are inefficient.

The most common reason for inefficiency is that the activities in the head office have developed in an uncoordinated way without design or challenge. This results in empire building, role duplication and departments creating little value.

If the roles in the structure are appropriate but are filled by staff with the wrong competencies, the work required will not be achieved. Alternatively, if the roles are not clearly defined, the work expected from the head office is also not achieved.

In organisations where the boundaries between operational work and head-office functions are not clear, the head-office roles are often dragged into operational decision-making, causing inefficiencies and damaging gaps in the strategic work the head office should be doing.

If the structure is inefficient, then the work it should do needs to be redefined through the organisation work design process, after which the new roles should be structured appropriately. This could mean that services are decentralised to operating units or outsourced.

A role of the corporate centre is to set the synergy rules for the organisation. These rules should make the ROI sum of the corporate model organisation greater than the sum of the individual business units in it if they are operated independently. Synergy rules are often described in policy statements within which all parts of the group must work. Some examples of activities that will be governed by synergy rules include:

- Controlling the allocation of capital for investment and the delivery of return on investment commitments.
- Having preferred suppliers for the organisation to ensure economies of scale in supplier contracts.
- Defining the management approach for key customers purchasing from several business units.
- Setting the activity parameters of each unit – whether business or service – to ensure that competition between units is not damaging.
- Setting values and ethical policies.
- Setting the policy for performance management, remuneration and bonus payments.
- Appointing business and service-unit leaders.
- Stipulating the image for the group such as brand identity.
- Setting internal cross-charging policies for commercial transactions within the organisation.
- Setting language policies.
- Setting IT policies.

The synergy rules also play a large part in creating the whole organisation's culture as they set many of the behavioural norms expected from the organisation. An approach to these policies involves producing innovative ways of working and challenging traditional norms and, if successful, can create a competitive advantage for the organisation.

MANAGING LARGER NUMBERS OF BUSINESS UNITS

The corporate model can be appropriate for very large organisations with many business and service units in many locations. A single centralised structure can manage a limited number of business units. As the numbers and complexity of the business units in the organisation increases, so too does the challenge of optimising synergies and performance management. If there are too many business units or the units are too complex, then another level of hierarchy to integrate this work is often required. This level is normally termed a region or a division. A multi-division form of an organisation is sometimes referred to as an M-Form organisation (Oliver Williamson).

A region or division is a lateral organisation design element that enables leadership of large spans of business units. In organisation design terms, it is an integrating element. This does not change the model itself. It is still a corporate model organisation but it does increase the leadership hierarchy. In this model, groups of business and service units will report into a divisional function rather than directly into the central function. There will be more than one divisional function and the divisional leadership will represent their business units in the central function.

These divisions play an integrating role that provides greater focused guidance to the units. The split of the divisions will be based on one of the design model options, such as customer, technology or geographic. The divisions will normally need their own service staff functions but adding an extra level to deal with scope complexity often adds to the complexity of managing the business in terms of decision-making and information flows.

The divisions do not duplicate the role of the corporate centre but focus on the activities that manage performance and support the business units within their portfolio. The functions within a division are normally a combination of information and analysis services that exist purely because of the division and centralised services used by all business units in the division.

The benefits of implementing divisions include improved synergy from the activities of the business units in the division due to the dedicated leadership and services allocated to it. Organisations will need more integration when they are growing or changing rapidly.

However, there is a cost to this extra level that the synergies need to outweigh. A poorly implemented divisional structure could lead to duplication of services, poor coordination with the rest of the business, and the central corporate strategic team losing touch with the activities and performance of the value-creating business units.

When lateral organisation designs are put in place, it creates an opportunity to view the organisation in a new way. The divisional focus does not have to be the same as the business units it manages, so it could be a geographic (as in a regional) structure within which product business units reside.

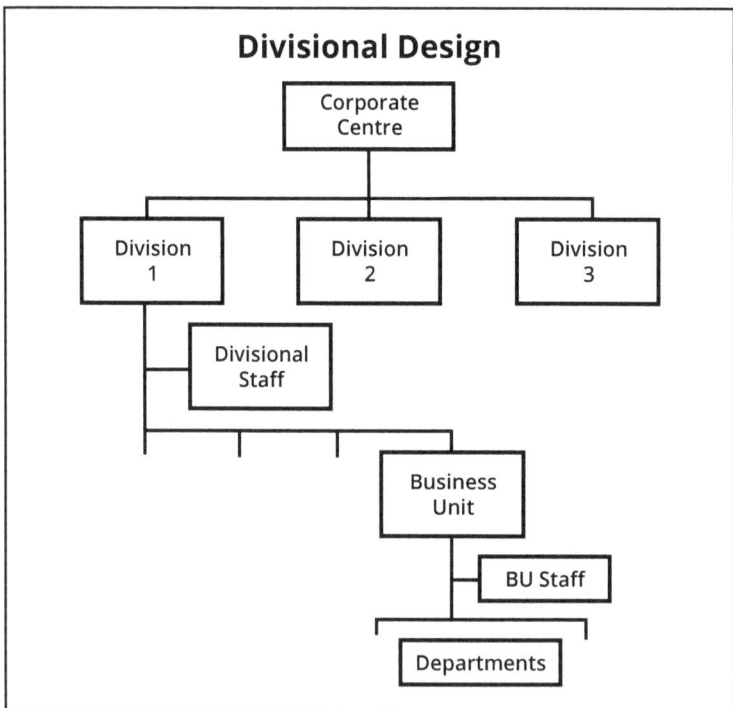

Divisional Design

WHY IS IT IMPORTANT TO TRY TO GET THE CORPORATE DESIGN RIGHT?

In a corporate design there is no single right design; it is a choice of how to achieve the work in the organisation and the design chosen will have its pros and cons compared with other options.

However, the corporate design can really support the strategic and competitive positioning of the organisation. For example, choosing the right customer segmentation for a business unit leads to the location of the products, the processes to produce them and the customer services to support them.

More challenges arise from further levels of design choices such as a geographic split. Does the organisation have a few large business units that will have economies of scale or many small ones that can be placed close to customers and spread the risk of any problem affecting production? Services can be placed in separate units in central structures or outsourced. An inappropriate design will lead to higher costs and slower delivery of services.

Divisions or regional centres support the management of complex organisations but create a barrier to the corporate centre from the value-creating business units. A poor design of a divisional structure will lead to reduced synergies and higher costs as divisions compete against each other. This can end in empire building and a culture that drags the division away from the centre.

Organisation designs need to reflect the market and how it changes over time. Car production has moved from 'any colour you want as long as it is black' (a product design pushed onto the market by Ford) to production lines where each car is custom-made for a specific customer.

Great designs can hugely influence the market. Companies like Dyson and Apple are dominating the marketplace with great products, as well as by how they have chosen the work their organisations must do internally and what must be outsourced. A company like Amazon has designed an organisation completely different to the traditional shops selling the same products. The design has been so radical that most of the traditional bookshops have now closed. The number of high-street bookshops halved in the the UK in the seven years up to 2012 due to the growing popularity of digital purchasing and e-books (as reported by *The Daily Telegraph*).

At a less radical level a better organisation design will play a huge part in differentiating the market leaders from the average organisations in the market. An effective organisation design will reduce comparative costs and through more effective processes increase the potential of the organisation to grow market share.

A corporate model should be able to deliver both customer proximity through business units and the economies of scale for both production volumes and costs of services that smaller competitors cannot match.

The challenge of the design is to adapt it as the organisation grows. Redesigning the organisation is the enabler of change, and in many organisations it feels as if change is constant. As new business units are acquired or new units are opened, a decision needs to be made as to whether to change the current organisation design. A larger organisation may lead to an opportunity to provide services differently, possibly through combining services from the units and transforming them into service centres. The acquisition of a new business unit may mean that the old and new units are reorganised into new units possibly with a different core design to the original ones. For example, two independent business units based on providing products to different regions might be restructured into three customer-focused units.

Each time the organisation grows, an opportunity arises to assess whether the current design is optimum for the new organisation.

New design opportunities also arise from new technologies and products, and the organisation's desire to enable strategies with linked designs.

BUSINESS MODELS FOR INTERNATIONAL ORGANISATIONS

Most corporate model organisations will have some form of international work so design options for international organisations are particularly important for this complexity of organisation.

The first organisation design choice for many organisations expanding internationally is to open a business unit that can focus on managing the specific needs of the stakeholders in the new country. The initial design of this unit is often a start-up but with resources the design could be more complex. The creation of a new business unit steps the overall organisation design into a corporate model if it was not already in this model. This means that the corporate model is the most common form of design if an organisation has international operations.

However, large international organisations with simple products or processes resulting in a low number of stakeholders can have a much simpler organisation design than one requiring lots of stakeholders. Some examples of well-known organisations with simple processes are Starbucks, McDonald's and Facebook.

Up until a few years ago a corporate model would be needed to manage the financial and business complexity of operating in multiple countries. This could be challenged as the internet facilitates the spread of even simpler models to multiple countries, streaming all income to a single point. Some internet-based organisations are transitioning through the stages of growth at a breathtaking pace, reaching global recognition and huge capital value in a few years. The speed at which digitally-based services can attract customers is phenomenal, with the same product or service for one person duplicated millions or billions of times, such as Twitter.

The lowest complexity for a global organisation is probably a mature business unit. This is because the range and complexity of stakeholders in a global organisation will be large and a minimum scale of organisation is necessary to support the expertise required to respond to these stakeholder demands.

An organisation applying the corporate model with operations in multiple international locations will tend to have some of the following characteristics:
- A simple and easily duplicated business model
- A simple product range
- The ability to outsource large parts of the value chain
- The customer interface channel is similar in all parts of the world
- Technology-enabled delivery of services
- It works within a single industry sector
- A dominant centre for leadership and control
- A few key centres of operations
- Minimal differences in regulation

A good example of this is McDonald's, which is represented in most world markets and has many employees. But it is a simple core business copied many times, with employees working in similar roles within similar outlets. Other household names, such as Apple or Nike, have kept their organisation designs simpler by outsourcing large parts of their potential value chain.

Most organisations requiring a complex international design model have the majority of their markets outside of their home country. This means that they need designs that reflect the challenges of working in multiple countries and cultures.

Many organisations of all sizes have international aspects to their business, such as selling to customers in different countries or sourcing suppliers from different markets. These organisations are sometimes termed transnational corporations. These interactions are relatively straightforward and do not add much complexity to the organisation. The impact of geographical locations on organisations has already been discussed; having locations in different countries is an extension of this model.

When an organisation decides to locate part of its business in another country the complexity of the organisation can rapidly increase as the number of stakeholder groups will also increase. To make the expansion attractive there are likely to be substantial synergies in stakeholder demand, especially customer demands but each major difference in stakeholder demand will add work and therefore costs to the organisation.

An organisation must understand how its design in the new country needs to be different to the one in the home country to deliver its value chain. Some of the issues facing an organisation expanding to a new country could be:
- The size of the potential market is not known
- Language and cultural differences
- The availability of competent staff
- Finding suppliers for the services required
- The difficulty of developing the brand and attracting customers
- Internal communication and information across multiple languages
- Aligning policies and processes for the financial legislation in the country, including tax and foreign exchange

The strategy of this organisation will also have to reflect external factors that could be different to the home country, such as:
- Economic stability
- Political stability
- Government support for business
- Logistics/utilities in a country – water, roads, towns, electricity
- Environmental conditions and climate

A move to an international model leads to a choice of what work to do in each business unit and the choice of whether to duplicate the business model in the home country or to try to gain a competitive advantage from locating parts of the value chain in other countries.

There are several choices to consider in the design of an international organisation:

1. THE SAME PRODUCT/SERVICE IN DIFFERENT LOCATIONS

The simplest form of geographic design is when all business units are similar in each geographic location, whether in different parts of the same country or in international locations. The same business model is duplicated. As mentioned, a good example of this would be McDonald's where the restaurants are similar all over the world.

A benefit of this approach is that it grows the potential market for the organisation's products and services. This benefit is especially relevant when current markets are becoming saturated or impacted by a downturn in the economy of the home country. The growth of locations spreads the risk of the impact of a downturn in a single market and allows some flexibility for a local approach to support customer differentiation. Increasing the locations, particularly into different cultures, makes the organisation more complex to manage and there are constant challenges between standardizing the international product and adapting it for local needs.

Duplicating the same organisation design in different countries should limit the potential risks of expansion. However, just because the offering is the same does not mean that the design will be of the same complexity. The stakeholders in the organisation will be different and they could demand different work from the organisation, which will need to be reflected in its design. Some of the challenges include:

Customers: Who buys a product from an organisation, how they buy it, when they buy it, and what else they buy with the product can change depending on location. Different cultures, demographics, choice of alternatives and economy all influence how customers buy products.

Employees: The number of staff required in an organisation depends on the competencies of available employees and the options available to buy in services. Lower levels of competencies normally mean smaller allocations of tasks per person and more supervision, which in turn lead to taller hierarchies. If services are not available to source into the organisation they must be supplied internally by the organisation, leading to more departments or service units, which also results in taller hierarchies.

Legal: Differences in trade regulations, business ownership rules, employment laws and trade laws will all influence the work in a business and how it is organised.

Suppliers: Most organisations rely on the support of a wide range of suppliers, and the design of an organisation in any location is a reflection of this support. High-quality supplier outsourcing of large volumes of non-core work allows the organisation design to be lean. If suppliers are not available, then the design will reflect much more in-house work.

Financial: The financial environment for the organisation can change through tax legislation, the currency used in the location, the strength of the economy, accounting regulations and corruption. How the organisation deals with these challenges will impact the design of the organisation.

Society: Society's perception of the organisation and its work will differ across locations. This will lead to different levels of acceptance and support for the organisation, which could influence its design. Other factors, such as the weather or time zones, could also influence when and how work takes place in the organisation.

These extra complexities will increase and change the work in the organisation, which will lead to higher costs and possibly different organisation designs. These changes to the home-country model need to be rewarded by increased income from the larger market. Further external challenges from weather, infrastructure, transport and security could also add complexity when trying to start a business in a new country.

2. SPLITTING UP THE VALUE CHAIN

Rather than just duplicating the business model into different geographical locations, international expansion offers an opportunity to change the organisation design to make it more competitive.

With more globalisation, organisations are locating different parts of their process in the most suitable international locations. In this approach the organisation will perform different activities in different international locations, for example, designing the product in the USA because of the high levels of design skills based there, manufacturing it in Mexico because the cost of labour is more competitive than the USA and then having sales and distribution channels in both markets. The model allows specialisation of skills in each location and optimises the skills of resources in different locations, which should provide overall economies of scale. However, this leads to a complex value chain to manage and puts the whole organisation at risk from possible non-performance in a few locations.

A variation of this model being applied more widely, particularly in the motor industry, is the placement of different products in various countries each supplying the global market. For example, if an organisation has three products, one is manufactured in the USA, another in Africa and the third in Asia. Large economies of scale can be gained in this approach but these need to be balanced by the risks of one country being unable to produce, and the challenge of standardising quality across different countries each with its own stakeholders.

OPTIONS WITHIN THESE TWO MODELS

In addition to choosing whether to do the same work in different countries or specialise activities in different countries, the organisation can choose what work should be done to manage these organisations and how the work will be delivered. When locating businesses internationally, the approach to that business can vary from a direct copy of the business in its country of origin to having broad parameters of the business concept that are implemented in each country, depending on that country's culture and market conditions.

If an organisation invests in a fully owned organisation in a new country, it will have the most control over this organisation and should reap all the rewards. But this approach can come with high costs and risks if the organisation is not sure that its business model is viable in that country or investment capital is scarce. Other approaches that reduce some of the risks and costs are to licence products to a local supplier, to offer franchise agreements where the buyer inputs some of the start-up capital, or to join with a local company in a partnership. If the new venture has its own legal standing with shareholders and a board separate to the country of origin, then the model of design is becoming a global one.

These choices influence the organisation's style of centralised management as well as whether it will have decentralised authority in its various locations. A highly centralised organisation will have high bureaucracy with rules and procedures that dictate how the international business must operate. A less centralised organisation will have a limited number of policies, such as ensuring the quality of a product or employment standards, but for many of the business activities, it can choose the best approaches for the local conditions even if they differ from those in the home country.

An organisation that applies the same business model to all its international operations will normally have a dominant management style based on the location of the parent company, and they apply this same style to all their organisations around the world. This has the advantage of standardisation, which should bring improved economies of scales and ease of control. The disadvantages will be a lack of flexibility to local conditions and cultures that could provide an advantage to local competitors.

Each country an organisation enters will bring its own challenges and the approach that works in one may not work in another. In international operations the design of work in an organisation is likely to vary in each location even if the product/service and technology applied are the same. The globalisation of work is a key driver in the need for complex organisation designs and the global design model is now needed in more much smaller organisations than in the past, thus becoming a more common model.

As organisations grow globally, they could become distant from their home country or their core geographical culture becomes blurred as influences from all around the world create a unique culture. This stateless organisation creates problems for tax, information security and legal regulation. Huge organisations like Apple or Google are already being challenged for their domicile for tax payments and their accountability to protect the information they hold concerning their international customers.

There are a few global organisations that are moving away from their national or cultural roots to form an organisation that becomes difficult to pin down to a country or regional culture. It is likely that this form of organisation will become more common in the future. These organisations will apply business philosophies appropriate to several cultures and mix and match the best approaches. Each of the operations will have a different culture aligned to their location and the optimum approaches for employees, government and customer service. The leadership team needs to also reflect this diversity and select a location for the parent company that is convenient for the organisation rather than loyalty to the country where it was founded.

A global organisation used to be a term restricted to the largest and most complex organisations in the world but this is changing as technology is transforming worldwide brand awareness.

134

TRANSITIONING FROM A CORPORATE TO A GLOBAL COMPANY MODEL

A different model is needed to direct an organisation with more than one corporate business model. The transition from a corporate model normally occurs through mergers or acquisitions of large corporate or mature business units.

The next model is a global model and it is characterised by a group strategic centre sitting above corporate business model organisations. A corporate model business joining a larger global model group would find little change in their model but there would be a level of leadership that monitors and guides the expectations of its board through setting profit dividends and the investment of capital parameters.

Google is a great example of a global business that is moving from a corporate model to a global model. Google has a dynamic history – an idea initiated in 1996 progressed to a start-up in a garage in 1998. By 2000 it was a growing basic management with 40 employees that rapidly grew to 800 employees by 2004. After buying Android in 2005, it grew so quickly that by 2012 it was global organisation utilising a corporate model to manage 37 000 employees. The $12.5 billion acquisition of Motorola Mobility in 2012 with its 16 000 employees required Google to run two separate corporate model businesses. It has chosen to run them separately rather than to integrate them.

In the first edit of this book I was going to leave the Google story at this point of transition but the world changes quickly. In August 2015 Google announced a big reorganisation, moving it to a global design model conglomerate. Larry Page and Sergey Brin will run a holding company called Alphabet. Within Alphabet there will be individual subsidiaries, such as moon projects, driverless cars and its original internet search and advertising business. Each of these will be separate companies applying the appropriate design model for their complexity.

MODEL 5: GLOBAL

A global organisation model is a design to manage several organisations of which at least one is seen as independent from a legal perspective, and at least one applies a corporate design model. This global model is most relevant when the various corporates fall into different industries and are under different regulatory governance. This regulatory governance could be due to national or regional legislation, which means that a separate governance board is required.

This level of organisational structure complexity has a global theme because it is the structure found in some of the world's largest organisations. Organisations of this complexity are frequently termed conglomerates – there is common ownership but few or no operating links between divisions or companies. Wikipedia has a list of 450 notable conglomerates in the world and this list will cover the majority of organisations with this global design. Only a select few organisations reach this level of complexity.

It is normal for most organisations with this design to have substantial business interests in multiple countries. An organisation applying the model does not have to trade internationally but it is rare for it not to do so. Many are so large that the corporate design organisations within them are individually listed on stock markets.

The global model is a model of organisation design that is applied when a business becomes too complex for the corporate model. If an organisation needs a more complex model than the corporate model, it must split its organisation into more than one corporate model, possibly also with some mature business units. In order to direct this type of organisation, a central high-level team is needed that is positioned above these corporate and business unit model organisations. This leadership design element can be termed a global strategic centre.

An organisation utilising this model would normally be a recognised brand in most parts of the world; it would have a large share of the global market for its product ranges and therefore have many customers. They will be very influential and powerful, with large balance sheets, and listed on at least one major stock exchange. They do not have to have a presence in every world market or have large numbers of employees but most do. It is the business world's equivalent of a government, with the organisations within it likened to government ministries. Many organisations utilising this model have turnovers greater than the GDP of many countries.

Many successful American companies have become global. Six of those in the top-10 largest by market value, including Google, sell more abroad than locally, and in almost all cases the proportion of their foreign-to-local sales is rising.

All the shares of the corporate model companies could be held by this central global parent company but this is not always the case. The parent company generates income from share dividends and fees, as well as the longer-term capital growth in share value of the businesses in the group.

The organisations utilising this global design need this structure because they cannot remain in the corporate model or there is little benefit to remaining in it even though it may be more cost-effective. This could be due to the following:
- The group may cover different industry sectors each with their own regulations. For example, in the UK there are several retail organisations that also own banking services. The banks are heavily regulated with their leaders needing approval from the banking regulator, so it will be standard practice that the bank and retail businesses are legally separated with their own individual boards.
- Geographical locations, each with their own regulations, legal systems and business traditions, often drive the need to separate organisations from the wider group through setting up the organisation in an applicable legal format

for that location, with a board or leadership framework matching the needs of local regulations. For example, some countries regulate foreign ownership of companies and so shareholding may have to be spread to local partners.

- If the group is made up of independent organisations with little synergy across their businesses, it may be the best option to run them as independent businesses.
- If the group is looking to divest a part of their business, they will want to set it up as a more independent organisation that can be easily separated from the rest of the group.
- If there are different investors in a part of the group, they will probably want their investment separated from the other organisations so that it can be ring-fenced and monitored. This normally means a separate legal entity with its own board on which the investors will be represented.

If this model is the most appropriate design, then it must create more value for investors than the sum of the unlinked corporate model organisations within it. Greater value can be created through an ability to raise cheaper finance because of scale, the protection of income streams through a more diverse portfolio, and some economies of scale for strategic services. A major benefit should come in the ability to attract more qualified strategic leaders and technical experts than the smaller parts of the organisation.

Organisations with this global model will be large, normally having between 10 000 and 200 000 employees and have a turnover measured in billions of dollars. These structures will normally develop from the growth of corporate organisations and acquisitions of either whole organisations or substantial shareholding. The leadership team needs to focus on macro-economic drivers, for instance optimising the value of the portfolio in the long run rather than focusing on running the individual organisations.

There are likely to be a few international competitor organisations of a similar size but more competition will take place in the markets of the corporate organisations within the group. The organisations will be very powerful and the growth of competitors of a similar size will therefore be infrequent.

The competitive edge of this organisation is its ability to leverage large capital resources to enter and influence markets and gain synergy from multiple investments in a global environment. Growth in a global organisation is normally through mergers and acquisitions as exposure to industries or markets is strengthened through the takeover of competitors. Equally important is to divest from an industry or market at the right time to optimise capital returns and minimise risks. The timeframe for a conglomerate is very long term. So, one of the key things that they can provide their subsidiaries is long-term capital. Warren Buffett says that his ideal holding period for an investment is 'forever'.

There will be many stakeholder groups in this organisation, including multiple international and society stakeholders. This means that the CEOs are often very high profile and influential in their industries and regions of operation. Because of their profile, these leaders, rather than the board, are often seen by observers as the organisation's ultimate decision-makers. If the CEO becomes too powerful and unduly influences a weak board, this can be damaging for the organisation.

Moving from a corporate to a global model could involve splitting a large corporate structure into two, or acquiring more corporate model organisations. Sometimes these large organisations with multiple corporate models are called a group. Each of these corporate models is relatively independent, with their own boards and regulatory accountability within their own sectors. Above these corporate structures a level of leadership needs to be created with its own board and normally a small strategically focused group head office. In this model there is a board of leaders who oversees a number of relatively independent organisations each with their own board. These two levels of boards, each with their own industry and regulatory accountability, are a key design element of this model.

The work required in a group strategic centre sits above work in the corporate model. This work is not to manage the organisation operationally or strategically. The accountability to manage the organisation sits in the lower model organisations.

The work in this new level of hierarchy above the corporate model organisation is highly strategic and long term. To satisfy investors and other stakeholders it needs a small structure that includes some competencies in corporate finance, merger and acquisitions, international tax, economic and market analysis, executive recruitment, public relations and investor communications. The leadership team in this parent structure manages a portfolio of shareholding in the corporate model organisations. They will normally have an infrequent influence on the individual organisations but the decisions will be significant, such as changing leadership, investing capital or the acquisition of a new organisation. They will focus on return on capital from their investments, thus influencing the most senior leadership positions in each corporate model organisation and divesting or investing in organisations for the long-term strength of the portfolio.

Some global organisations also implement certain centralisation of services for all organisations in the group. However, too much centralisation of services could lead to the global model reverting to a corporate model.

A holding company can be a form of global design. It can be the approach applied for investing in several corporate organisations but it is more 'arm's length' in its influence than a central global structure. A holding company is one that holds large shareholdings of large organisations but it has limited direct influence over their management. The term holding company usually refers to a company that does not produce goods or services itself; rather, its purpose is to own shares of other companies. It is a simpler business model that makes money from shareholding purchases and divestments rather than offering organisation leadership. This differentiation is often blurred as large shareholding does lead to a large influence on strategic direction.

Berkshire Hathaway in the United States is the largest publicly traded holding company globally; it owns shares in many companies giving it the ability to influence not only these companies but also whole markets. In 2011 Berkshire Hathaway influenced 70 subsidiaries, employing more than 250 000 people, through the firm's headquarters, which employs a little over 20 people.

Currently this global model is the highest level of organisational complexity that can be generically achieved

The best example of the global organisation model is probably General Electric. Thomas Edison, the founder of General Electric, made it into a conglomerate through his obsession to change the world through electricity. In 2008 it was the 10th largest company in the world, with 390 000 employees, 215 manufacturing plants in the US and 80 more in 20 other countries, and 100 laboratories. It is a highly decentralised company with more than 300 operating departments and service components. Each of these departments is run as if it were a separate company and they are organised into 10 operating groups.

Modern-day tech billionaires are using the cash they have created from initial great ideas into conglomerate betting on further new ideas that may change the world. Google has invested in artificial meat, Amazon in drones and Facebook in virtual-reality equipment. An exciting trend is an investment in space transport by Virgin, Google and Tesla CEO Elon Musk, which potentially could lead to a space-based organisational design.

Some of the largest organisations are now state-controlled, especially those in countries with a communist foundation, such as Russia's Gazprom, an energy firm run by the Russian Government, or China's PetroChina and China Mobile. The control and governance of these organisations is often unclear; even thought they may have a leadership board, final decisions on their activities are frequently made at the highest levels of government.

CHANGING THE DESIGN MODEL

At any point in time, an organisation will be positioned in one of the model designs and its leadership will need to decide whether it should stay in the current model, grow into the next design model or, if times are hard, revert to a lower model. From an organisation design perspective, an organisation may have a vision of a model it would like to achieve in the future but should focus its strategy on only the next model up or down to its current model. Once this move to the next model is achieved, the organisation can develop a new strategy to further step-up models.

STAY THE SAME SIZE

A leadership team can review the resources available to an organisation and the market opportunities at any stage, and decide that growth to the next level of strategic model is not an attractive strategy. In a study of 100 companies that have been in business for more than 100 years, 89.4% employed less than 300 people. This seems to suggest that the option to become more effective in their current design model was a successful strategy for many organisations.

Some of the reasons to stay at the same level of design complexity could be:
- Leadership and the main stakeholders are happy with the results and culture of the current organisation.
- The necessity to mature in the current level of complexity if the organisation has only recently moved into it.
- The competitive advantage offered by having a restricted size, for example, where premium prices are achieved from luxury goods due to limited supply.
- A restriction on resources to enable growth, such as the availability of specialist skills.
- Leadership is comfortable controlling a business of the current size and wishes to keep it that way.

- The economy or other external factors make the risks associated with growth and the change it involves too great for the potential benefits.
- Funding for growth is not available.

In order to make the organisation more effective in its current size, there are a number of options, including the following:
- Process improvement to make the business more efficient.
- Employee development to improve competencies, creating multi-skilling and team flexibility.
- Investment in capital assets to keep up to date with modern technology.
- Deepening customer relationships to sell more products.
- Increasing marketing spend to develop the brand.
- Developing new products or services.
- Partnering with other organisations to make the organisation more efficient or to strengthen the customer proposition.

Once an effective organisation design has been achieved, which creates superior returns on investment, it is risky to move to a new, more complex design. Staying the same size with gradual improvements can create the best long-term value. Many mergers and acquisitions fail to deliver greater value than the combined value of the pre-merged smaller organisations.

GROW TO THE NEXT MODEL

Although there are benefits to not growing, it can be viewed as strategically unexciting. In many parts of the world there is a dominant strategic view that growth is good to the point that it is necessary for survival. The majority of strategies tend to focus on organisational growth, the benefits of which include the following:

Fewer similar competitors: At each stage of growth there are fewer organisations of a similar size in the market. The competitive challenge will be different at each level as the markets will be larger.

Most small organisations have a local focus for their market which, as they grow, becomes regional, national, international and possibly global. Organisations normally enter each of these new markets with a low market share which, if they are successful, will grow to allow them to break into a larger market. The attraction of moving into a bigger market is the extended customer base with the potential for larger financial returns that reward the organisation for becoming more complex.

Economies of scale: Growth should create a cost and production capacity advantage. If costs can be spread across a larger volume of businesses and income bases, then the cost per unit of the product or service will drop. This should place a large organisation at an advantage to a smaller one, as they should be able to produce the items in question more cheaply.

Financial options for investment: A small organisation normally has to rely on an owner to fund the initial investment to start up an organisation and prove its viability. As an organisation grows, other funding sources will become available from investors and banks, and security for this lending will move from the owner's personal assets to the organisation's assets, such as its lending capital. Larger organisations can raise investment funds from share listing or interest-bearing products, such as bonds, with these products becoming more international as the organisation becomes global.

More stability enabling a longer-term perspective: For a small organisation a few days without income can be disasterous. As organisations grow they can begin to benefit from longer timeframes of performance as long as no disasters occur. This longer-term view allows for recruitment to prepare for growth, larger IT systems, building a brand, research and development, and growth into new markets. These investments should provide a larger organisation with a competitive advantage and the ability to prepare for economic and market changes.

Promotions and job security: A growing organisation will generally provide employees with more job security and opportunities for personal growth. A larger organisation should be strong enough to survive more challenges than a smaller one, and an increase in roles creates opportunities for promotion.

These benefits of growth are normally linked to internal challenges that make an organisation difficult to manage. The table below shows the drivers of change when an organisation needs to consider moving to a more complex organisation design model.

The need to transition up to the next model is normally reflected by evidence that the current design is inefficient for the needs of the growing organisation. Some of these symptoms reflecting a need to move up to the next model are shown in the following table.

Model change	Symptoms supporting a need for change
Start-up to basic management	The leaders/entrepreneurs are spending long hours outside of work hours catching up with the work required to manage the business. Management work is not conducted efficiently as there is confusion over decision-making and accountabilities in the team. Increased volumes of work require more focus on the policies, systems and processes to apply, and dedicated management time is needed to implement them.
Basic management to mature	Functional stakeholders require complex outputs or take up too much time, and specialists need to be employed to deliver this work. Due to the volume of work, it becomes more cost-effective to employ staff to deliver services previously outsourced. Growth is being constrained due to not having the resources to design and implement strategies for new products or markets. Systems for control and information management need to become more complex in each function.

Model change	Symptoms supporting a need for change
Mature to corporate	Leadership spends too much time managing short-term operational issues and there is little time for strategy. Profitability management is poor as all decisions impacting profits are taken by the central leadership. The organisation is slow to respond to localised customer demands. Policies and processes designed for the whole organisation are inhibiting the performance of minority value chains.
Corporate to global	Stakeholders question whether governance is effective in a corporate model due to the diverse nature of the portfolio. There is a risk to the whole group if legal separation is not implemented between organisations in the group.

Growth has substantial benefits but it also has potential downsides for an organisation. The first challenge will be the cost of implementing the growth – it will lead to higher costs in the short term until revenues and profitability returns are achieved A rapidly growing organisation that has borrowed to fund an investment could be limited in its options to respond to market changes.

The management of each growth stage becomes more complex, requiring different management practices to plan, control and direct the organisation. This bureaucracy can be inefficient and increase costs in excess of any benefit created. As the organisation grows, it could lose its entrepreneurial culture as the formalisation of work rules inhibits flexibility to changing customer needs. Many large organisations are slow to change due to the cost and complexity of turning the organisation in a new direction.

With growth there will be a greater distance between leadership decisions and the delivery of value to customers. If the organisation cannot spot changing customer trends, it will provide an opportunity for smaller, more flexible competitors to enter the market. Larger organisations become more of a focus for society stakeholders and regulators, which can add costs to stakeholder management that smaller competitors do not have.

Growing too large within each design model will also cause problems with which the organisation model may not be able to cope – a significant driver to change to a more complex model. You need to change the model when the current design is not delivering the work required to satisfy the stakeholders in the organisation. Each model overcomes problems of too much growth in the model below it. The basic business model creates more management structure to the start-up model. The mature business model reflects this growth of structure with the functional teams an organisation needs. A large, single business unit could struggle to align itself to customer segments and a corporate model of multiple business units can overcome this problem as each unit focuses on its own customer segments. At a global level the parent organisation can support each corporate to deliver society stakeholder interests.

Ultimately, an organisation that fails in its growth strategy may have to revert to its previous, less complex design model.

CONTRACT TO A LOWER ORGANISATION DESIGN MODEL

For some organisations contracting down to the model below is preferable to growing a strategic solution. This decision is, however, normally a step back for the organisation, resulting from an unsuccessful strategy, a loss of market share to competitors, or unfavourable economic conditions. The lower complexity model will have less stakeholders and therefore less costs.

A global business contracting to a corporate model would decide on its core corporate business and then divest from the other corporate businesses in the group. This approach would save little in costs to the core corporate business but would release capital from the non-core business, which should provide some financial security to the remaining core. With only one corporate business the global centre structure would not be needed and would be combined into the leadership of the smaller corporate business.

A similar approach would be applied for reducing the complexity of a corporate model business to a mature business unit model. It would sell or close some business units and combine the remaining business units into a single unit. This centralisation of control could be advantageous as it would reduce duplicated costs especially in the management hierarchies and service elements previously residing across several business units.

A mature business unit can simplify its model by reducing its number of employees and outsourcing services that are no longer required on a permanent basis within the organisation. Without teams to manage, management roles will be reduced and the organisation will reflect a basic management model.

In survival mode, a basic management model reverts to a start-up model as the manager/leader role returns to directly creating value and the number of employees is reduced to a single team.

TRANSITIONING TO A NEW DESIGN MODEL

The point at which an organisation changes to a new model of complexity, whether up or down, is a transition point as it represents a significant change to how the organisation will be managed. These transitions can happen very quickly, especially when an organisation is rapidly growing, or they evolve over many years as the work in an organisation slowly changes.

Transitioning between models is a turbulent time for any organisation. Senior roles change, work is reallocated and restructuring causes uncertainty across all impacted roles. Once implemented, it takes time to realign systems, processes and competencies to the new design, which can lead to a period of underperformance placing more pressure on the organisation. The size of the change to the previous design will proportionally increase the risks associated with the change.

The transition from a start-up entrepreneurial model to a basic business model requires the creation of full-time leadership positions from a collaborating team culture. This is often a stressful time for individuals who are either not chosen for this leadership role or realise that although they had many of the ideas to set up the organisation they were not suited to be the manager to take it forward. The more formal leadership role in a basic management model needs to bring more structure to the business to enable it to grow and align to a growing stakeholder base. This more formal approach can change the culture of the organisation, which may lead to some team members leaving, especially if the choice of leader does not have unanimous support.

As an organisation transitions from a basic management to a mature business, it is a time when a leader has to rely on more independent actions of their leadership team. For the leader this can be a point where they can no longer know everything happening in an organisation. It is a change from managing with hands-on knowledge to managing through information and a leadership team. It is a time for career opportunities, for promotion to leadership positions for team members or recruiting more formal management competencies into the organisation. A mature business unit will feel more formal as it will need to be relatively bureaucratic to deliver work to a wide range of new stakeholders, many of whom may be very bureaucratic, such as government departments and auditors.

Growing from a mature business to a corporate business is a major change for an organisation. The need for multiple business units creates an opportunity to implement appropriate policies and processes in each to enable further growth. The major design change is the creation of a centralised element above the business units: this can be as simple as the appointment of a few key leaders to a complex head office and service structure. In this design, decisions around the appropriate amount of centralisation and decentralisation of control will become more pressing. In this model there are often flows of change between greater amounts of either centralised or decentralised control as the organisation tries to position itself to stakeholder needs.

A change to a global structure from a corporate structure is probably the least disruptive within an organisation as the main impact will only be on the most senior leadership roles. However, each organisation will need to change to a strategy aligned to the expectations of the global parent. The global centre, after influencing the appointment of the boards and CEOs, normally plays little part in the operations of each corporate organisation to deliver profits. At intervals, normally through strategic planning, the global centre will influence the performance of the whole group through setting profit expectations, allocating capital, changing leadership, providing strategic services and creating a group profile in the market.

150

These transition points are frequently reached through organic growth and are not planned as formal events. Some periods of transformation can take years when the organisation is in a grey area of design between models. When a transition is required as a one-off event is when it is used to enable a new strategy, for instance when it's due to a merger or acquisition.

OBSERVING THE MODELS WITHIN LARGER ORGANISATIONS

Each large organisation is made up of a mixture of the smaller organisation designs. These can be organisations with the potential to stand alone as a business unit, or income or cost centre, and within each of these multiple departments and teams exist.

Within the largest organisation you can find all the other models in their almost pure context, thus a global organisation will be made up of several corporate organisations. Each corporate organisation will have mature businesses as business units and then within these there will be departments (led by managers), which will function in a similar way to a basic management model, and within departments there will be teams. The sub-organisations will exhibit some of the same criteria as an independent organisation of their complexity. This means that the systems, structure, technology and work flows will be similar but the number of stakeholders will be lower for sub-organisations within the larger organisation giving them a lower cost.

It is possible to analyse a large organisation through understanding the sub-organisations. In a large organisation the allocation of activities is based on the optimal mix for the organisation as a whole and it may not be possible to try and optimise each model within the whole.

The history of large organisations can also be reviewed through an assessment of how they have grown through these models as described in the following sub-section.

EXAMPLES OF ORGANISATIONS THAT ACHIEVED GLOBAL RECOGNITION AND HOW THEY GREW THROUGH THE MODELS

Not many organisations grow through these five models of design. The vast majority of organisations will not go – or have not yet gone – through these stages of growth. In the UK 95% of all businesses have less than 10 employees, placing them into the start-up or basic management model categories. A further 4% have between 10 and 50 employees – the vast majority of these will use the basic management model.

In the UK approximately 25% of these businesses are connected to real estate and renting, and a further 21% are involved in construction in other countries. The sectors will reflect the country's economic drivers but the majority of organisations in a country will be small.

This means that in the UK only 1% of organisations will need business designs that are more complex than the basic management model, but according to a survey in 2013 by Mintel this 1% accounts for two thirds of the value of all organisations in the UK. Out of this 1% only a handful of organisations will grow to need corporate or global design models.

Going back in history, there were few examples of complex business organisations before the Industrial Revolution. There were large organisations but these were either governmental, religious or military. Many of the designs used by large organisations have been proved to be successful in these organisations for hundreds of years.

It could be argued that tried-and-tested military structures are closely correlated to these five stages of design. A comparison could look like this:

- Platoon – start-up
- Company – basic management
- Regiment/battalion – mature business
- Division/army group – corporate
- Multiple army groups in different geographical locations and directed by central government decision making – global

Some of the largest and most complex organisations in the world today are still linked to governments, for instance, the armed forces, publically funded organisations such as NASA, and the National Health Service in the UK.

The dominant Western view of organisations is that strategies should enable growth, but many of these successful organisations optimise their current model and have no appetite for growth. This is one of the key strategic choices for leaders to make in an organisation.

The longevity of many organisations has been dictated by when the products and services they sell became possible. Many of the oldest organisations in the world are invariably linked to food, beverages and hospitality. Throughout history travellers sought out these necessities. A good example is the Grolsch Brewery, which was founded in the Netherlands in 1615.

The necessity for innovative technology has always been a catalyst for the formation of organisations – this hasn't changed for centuries. For example, the firearms company Beretta was established in Italy in 1526, and Cambridge University Press was founded in 1534.

Generally, though, before the Industrial Revolution there were few large organisations apart from military, religious and government. In the 17th century increasing global trade led to the emergence of banking and insurance organisations such as C. Hoare & Co, the UK's oldest family-owned private bank in 1672, and Lloyd's of London in 1688. The emergence of more banks in the late 17th and early 18th centuries such as the Bank of Scotland in 1695 and Barclays Bank in 1736* provided a financial foundation for the Industrial Revolution in the UK. The growth of the latter global organisation is summarised below, showing its approximate steps through the organisation design models.

153

BARCLAYS BANK	
Start-up	Goldsmith Bankers established in 1690.
Basic Management	In 1736 James Barclay joined as a partner of Goldsmith Bankers based at 54 Lombard Street, London, at which time Barclays become associated with a name in the banking sector.
Mature Business	In 1896 several banks in London and Provinces united under the banner of Barclays & Co, a joint stock bank.
Corporate	The bank expanded between 1905 and 1924 through amalgamations and acquisitions of other banks.
Global	It started to develop internationally, and differentiated the business from 1965 when it established the Barclays Bank of California; in 1966 it launched Barclaycard. In 2009 it had 4 750 branches in 50 countries.

*In 1736 James Barclay became a partner of the bank that was founded in 1690 by John Freame and Thomas Gould. At the time they were trading as Goldsmith Bankers.

With international trade, the first large commercial organisations, such as the East India Company, emerged. The Industrial Revolution developed due to new sources of power that could be applied to industrial innovation. New machines led to mass production in factories and the urbanisation of previously rural workers. As industries and global trade grew into the 19th century, so did the banks and insurance companies.

Engineering inventions that resulted from the Industrial Revolution have changed the world. A few of the most successful from that era still exist as global organisations today. General Electric saw exceptional growth in the 19th century as a result of the invention of the incandescent electric light bulb in 1878 in Thomas Edison's laboratory. It grew to a corporate model by 1892, and by 1895 it had expanded into a global model with business diversification, including building the world's largest locomotives. In 1896 it was one of the original 12 companies listed on the newly formed Dow Jones Industrial average. Innovations with a monopoly on functionality have been the fastest growers, as the new products have very clear benefits and instant demand.

A modern example of engineering innovation rapidly leading to a global organisation is Dyson, which manufactures electric appliances. Its growth, also from a start-up in an invention laboratory, is shown in the following table.

	DYSON
Start-up	From 1970 to 1993 inventor James Dyson worked from his laboratory developing products, including the sea truck and ball wheelbarrow before inventing his famous vacuum cleaner.
Basic Management	Investment allowed Dyson to skip this model.
Mature Business	In 1993 Dyson had the resources to open his own research centre and vacuum-cleaner factory.
Corporate	By 1995 Dyson was the UK's highest selling vacuum cleaner and its research centre had 350 engineers.

	DYSON
Large corporate design organisation with a global reach	In 2013 Dyson had achieved £6 billion in sales of designed products worldwide, including washing machines and hand dryers.

New cities enabled mass consumer demand for products which, by the early 20th century, had created some household names that still dominate the market today such as Coca-Cola and Heinz. However, their growth as shown below took decades.

	COCA-COLA	HEINZ
Start-up	Invented in 1886 by John Pemberton.	Henry John Heinz, born in 1844, started to sell farm produce from the age of 8. By the age of 16 Henry had several employees and sold produce to Pittsburgh grocers. Then he went to business college.
Basic Management	In 1888 it was bought by Asa Giggs Chandler who formed the Coca-Cola Company.	In 1869 Heinz formed a partnership selling bottled horseradish.
Mature Business	Business grows in the USA.	In 1888 it was reorganised into HJ Heinz Company selling ketchup and pickles. The phrase '57 Varieties' was coined in 1892.

	COCA-COLA	HEINZ
Corporate	By 1895 Chandler had built three syrup plants in Chicago, Dallas and Los Angeles, with sales to two bottlers, and by 1900 the drink was introduced to the UK.	By 1900 the company was incorporated and sold more than 200 products, including soup and beans. By 1905 the first factory was opened in England. In 1919 when Henry died Heinz had 6 500 employees and 25 factories.
Large corporate design organisations with a global reach	By 1920 there were 1 000 bottlers in the USA. Support for soldiers in World War II introduced Coke to the world, and now 1 billion drinks are consumed a day in 200 countries.	From 1949 major international expansion and acquisitions took place. Now Heinz employs 32 500 people and owns 150 number-one or -two brands worldwide. In 2013 it was purchased by the conglomerates Berkshire Hathaway and 3G Capital.

Technology in the 20th century has changed our world with many global organisations having their foundations in the first half of this century: Ford gave us the mass-produced motor car and Disney transformed entertainment. These two organisations revolutionised the way we perceived transport and entertainment, two of the key enablers to the rapid acceptance of new products and services around the world, and therefore the more rapid growth of global organisations.

Organisations building on physical products with other competitors will grow more slowly as they require time to build market share and expand manufacturing capacity. Time is needed to produce, distribute and sell, which limits the speed of growth, and the growth time-lag provides a window of opportunity for copycat competitors to set up markets, creating competition that limits the size of the global organisation.

Organic growth cannot miss out an organisation model but growth backed by investment can jump bands. Sometimes an organisation model is missed out if resources, especially financial, allow a good idea to be implemented in a relatively large organisation. An example of this is Dyson – it built a vacuum cleaner factory shortly after the innovation of the product design, therefore missing the basic management model. The most common model to miss out is the start-up model when the resources available allow the first model applied to be a basic management model.

It is feasible for an organisation to be created at any of the models of complexity. Anglo American was initiated as a corporate organisation in 1917 after raising £1 million in capital to invest in South African gold mining. By 1930 it was a global design organisation with investments in gold, platinum, diamonds and chemicals, as well as expanding into more African countries. Anglo American Platinum is the world's primary producer of platinum and was formed as a corporate model through Anglo American listing its platinum operating division separately. Toyota vehicles were formed as a division of Toyota Automatic Loom Works in 1933. The division was supported by the Japanese government and it was devoted to the production of automobiles. The first cars and trucks were produced in 1935 to US designs. Toyota Motor Corporation was established as a separate corporate model business. In 1937 it produced trucks in the war (with China) and cars again by 1947. During the 1960s it became a global organisation as it expanded to Brazil, Thailand and the US with 10 million units produced. The first car produced by Toyota outside of Japan was in Australia in 1963.

	TOYOTA
Start-up	
Basic Management	
Mature Business Unit	
Corporate	Formed as a division of Toyota Automatic Loom Works in 1933. The division was supported by the Japanese government and devoted to the production of automobiles. First cars and trucks produced in 1935 to US designs. Toyota Motor Corporation was established as a separate business in 1937. It produced trucks in the war and resumed manufacturing cars by 1947.
Global	By the 1960s Toyota had expanded to Brazil, Thailand and US with 10 million units produced. The first car produced outside of Japan was in Australia in 1963.

Retailing is a good example of how work is changing. Several organisations started in the late 19th century as department stores became fashionable for servicing the retail needs of towns and cities. Marks & Spencer, one of the larger retail groups in the UK, was started by Michael Marks as a market store in 1884. This start-up model grew to a basic management model as the number of stalls increased and was a mature business model by 1901. The organisation became more diversified with stalls, warehouses and offices in place, and the first shopping arcade shop opened. As the work became more complex, the business is likely to have become a corporate model when it was publically listed on the stock exchange in 1926 and continued in this model for several decades as it expanded. Between 1975 and 1990 Marks & Spencer's began to expand internationally; they opened stores in Europe after which they purchased Brooks Brothers and Kings Food Markets online in the US, as well as opening stores in Hong Kong. This international expansion and investments in banking and energy products required a move to a global organisation design.

The growth through the models that took Marks & Spencer nearly 100 years is under challenge from new retailers optimising modern technologies. It could be claimed that Amazon has created a new organisation design that has transformed the retail industry. Its initial focus on books, music and movies devastated the retail market selling these products as more customers bought online. The move into a broad range of goods, downloading, and the sale of specialist tablets and readers mean that it continues to be an innovative market leader. Goods can be offered 24 hours a day 365 days a year with a system that provides a tailored service with unique recommendations for each customer, and market-leading ease-of-purchase through 'One Click'.

Amazon was formed as a start-up in 1994 by Jeffrey P. Bezos and started selling books on the web in 1995. By 1997 it grew to a mature business model with 158 employees before it commenced a period of huge growth leading to over 56 000 employees in 2011. It has two areas of operational focus, ie North America and international, and plans to continue its growth in the latter markets. In 15 years Amazon has grown from a start-up to a worldwide household name. The Alibaba Group in China has taken a similar business model to Amazon and expanded from being a business–to-business portal for the Chinese market into a huge organisation.

Digital products such as e-books and movie downloads are different to manufactured products in that once produced they can be accessed by millions of people instantly. This allows the steps between growth models to speed up. A dramatic change in technology such as digital access can change the game for organisations designed for a market requiring the physical sale of products. New designs will be less complex and this lowered cost enables them to charge less giving them a competitive edge. The organisations worst off will be the ones with a need to maintain old traditional approaches yet compete with new technology as their costs will be extremely high.

In the late 20th and early 21st centuries, the speed of growth for some organisations rapidly increased as technology allowed for the immediate delivery of new products and services. Start-up to global dominance can now take a few years for internet and digital organisations, and the speed of this growth can lead to huge market shares for their niche markets.

This transformation of communication through social media is creating new business models with simple designs serving vast numbers of users and creating huge capital values. The most prominent of these is Facebook. Facebook was launched in 2004 as a start-up by students at Harvard University and by 2011 (with only 3 200 employees) it had one billion users that had delivered $3.7 billion in revenue. This organisation has moved very quickly through the stages from start-up to corporate.

Other organisations are growing in the same fashion. Twitter was founded in 2006, and by 2008 this start-up only had eight employees. It had a mature business model by 2012 with 900 employees, 300 million users and $145 million in turnover. Similar well-known organisations have small numbers of employees but a huge number of users, such as LinkedIn with less than 2 000 employees, and Spotify with 300 in 2012.

Internet-based organisations are creating a new phenomenon in organisation design, and it's one of huge perceived financial value and requiring only a relatively simple organisation design. The value is in the intellectual capital and brand not in the physical assets of the organisation. In each of these examples a simple product is sold globally to millions if not billions of users. The complexity of stakeholders is low as each customer is similar; which means that although the numbers of transactions are vast there is little variety to manage.

Although the business models of these organisations may be simple, the complexity of some of the work in these organisations is likely to be very high, as technology is creating the value for the organisation that would have required tens of thousands of junior employees in a more traditional organisation. The employees in these organisations are focused on global sales, designing leading edge IT systems, international corporate governance and system operations. To a certain extent the organisations are the top levels of the work required of any organisation with this volume of turnover.

However, these new companies often have relatively few employees, simple products duplicated millions of times, and therefore fewer stakeholder groups. These organisations with their relatively simple business models can become global household names worth billions with relatively simple designs compared with more traditional organisations. This makes them simpler organisations in terms of design resulting in global organisations with mature business unit or corporate design models. These more cost-effective organisation designs can change markets by undercutting the higher-cost, more complex designs of their more traditional global competitors. This benefits the consumer but withdraws from the industry huge amounts of potential income.

As we look to the future, more organisations are likely to grow very rapidly and leverage computer power rather than human labour to recreate industries that have been stable since the Industrial Revolution. Industries currently facing this challenge include not only retailers but also banking and media. The largest change in the future could be in manufacturing, with innovations such as 3D printing technology leading to new high-value businesses with simple structures that enable many customers to make their own products in their homes rather than buying those manufactured in factories. This new technology could have as large an impact on the world and the design of organisations as the Industrial Revolution did.

Complex structures are normally large employers and therefore good for the economy. There is a risk that these new organisations with their simple structures and high capital worth will destroy traditional markets and the employment that goes with them.

SUMMARY

As an organisation grows and becomes more complex it will need to be designed in a manner that delivers the work its stakeholders require. The typical growth steps in an organisation's design can be defined in five broad organisation models. These models reflect the challenges of managing and delivering increasing quantities of work.

Each model is a step up in design complexity to reflect the complexity of growth within the organisation. The design elements are the building blocks of a design and they increase in number as the organisation grows. The main design element is the business unit as this is the point where value is created for the organisation. In the first three models the growth in complexity is reflected within a single business unit. In the corporate and global models there are multiple business units. The design options increase as the models become more complex with multiple business units.

As the organisation becomes more complex, the choice of design has a bigger potential impact on the performance of the organisation. A more effective design for delivering work to stakeholders can achieve a significant competitive advantage for an organisation just as a poor design could lead to failure.

There are many examples of organisations growing through these models. Large corporate and global organisations can trace back their roots through these models, many back to a garage or market stall where the start-up team first initiated the organisation that became a global brand.

SECTION 3

IMPLEMENTING DESIGNS

INTRODUCTION

This section looks at practical ways to implement these models into an organisation's design. Moving to another design model is a major change for an organisation and this change brings with it risks to the stability of the organisation that could outweigh any benefits. However, many organisations have to adapt, and strategies will not be achieved if the organisation design model does not support it.

The first part of this section focuses on the reasons why it is appropriate to change the model of an organisation and leadership's role in the decision-making process. It offers an overview of the steps required to formulate and implement a new design.

DECIDING THE SCOPE OF AN ORGANISATION DESIGN PROCESS

It is a leader's role to design the organisation that will most effectively deliver the work to compete in its chosen market. The delivery of work in an organisation drives both cost and income and it is the reason why the organisation exists.

An organisation's design reflects how its leadership wants it to operate. There are choices of where and how value is created in an organisation and what services are required to support this value creation. As an organisation become larger and more complex, the variety of options increases. The split of work to different elements of an organisation is influenced by leadership's view of how work should be conducted in the organisation. What activities to centralise or decentralise are fundamental design choices for all models, as accountabilities and responsibilities need to be allocated to team members even in a start-up model.

The major reason for changing a design is when the work required in the organisation is not being effectively achieved. This may be because there is too much work or too little work, or the work is changing, either because current stakeholders want different work or the organisation sees an opportunity to attract new stakeholders. Leaders need to assess the external environment for new opportunities to make the organisation more competitive. The globalisation of trade and powerful IT systems provide greater flexibility for the location of work; they are also changing the face of many industries which results in new organisation designs. The organisation's approach to delivering new opportunities or reacting to threats is described in its strategy.

If the strategy of an organisation changes, then this could impact the design of the organisation. An organisation design should reflect and enable the desired strategy of the organisation. If an organisation's strategy changes, then a new design aligned to this strategy can create a catalyst for change to emphasise the importance of the new approach. An organisation requiring a customer-centric strategy would be likely to have customer-defined teams and business units. An organisation whose strategy is to grow sales in China could segregate these activities into a business unit to achieve this so that its progress towards this goal can be easily monitored.

If an organisation chooses a growth strategy, it needs to plan and prepare the organisation for the next level of organisational complexity from the model it is currently applying. There could be a vision to grow even larger but it is rare for a step through the models of growth to be missed. The challenge of moving to a new model of organisation design involves great change and risk to the organisation, as leadership roles, policies, systems and culture will all be impacted. It is important for an organisation to recognise if it is moving to a new level of model in its strategy so that it can prepare for these changes and appreciate their consequences.

Normally a design process is chosen by the organisation's leaders to support their strategy but sometimes a new design is forced onto an organisation through one of the following drivers of change.
- **A new parent company (larger organisation) takes control of the organisation.** The parent may decide to let the

organisation function as in the past or see the acquisition as an opportunity to improve the organisation's performance through a new design, or integrate it for synergy purposes with other organisations that the new parent already controls.

- **The development of a new greenfield operation** means that this new organisation needs to be designed either as a copy of existing operations or from first principles.
- **Uncontrollable external pressures** such as government legislation forcing processes to change.
- **The organisation acquires or merges with another organisation.** This always leads to a redesign of at least part of the organisation. The design is needed to integrate the work of the new organisation into the original one. The change could be as simple as the addition of a new business unit to the portfolio, which has little impact on the rest of the organisation, to a major change, which moves the model of the whole organisation to a new level and so impacts the work and processes throughout the organisation.

A new design normally supports the desired strategy and so follows the organisation's strategy process. If the strategy is not competitive, ie is without effective technology, processes, products and market positioning, it is unlikely that the organisation design is going to have a major impact on its performance.

However, sometimes the designs themselves are a strategic solution and lead other aspects of the strategy. In this case a significant competitive advantage is gained through a design that changes the market. Such a design might enable the application of technology to change traditional approaches to the market or move the organisation to a location that achieves a substantial cost advantage over competitors.

An effective organisation design needs to be balanced through a good appreciation of the strategy, the organisation's resources/

assets and what the stakeholders want from an organisation now and in the future. To commence a new organisation design, the following inputs are required from the leadership of an organisation:

- A clearly defined competitive strategy, which the design will need to support.
- Specified work activities that will deliver the strategy of the organisation and its desired performance targets.
- Value-chain technical processes that are optimum for market conditions.
- A competitive market strategy.
- A set of design criteria to use as the mandate for the design based on an understanding of stakeholder needs.
- Leadership support and commitment to the design process.
- The resources to follow through the design.

The internal and external drivers of change will dictate the scope and extent of design change on the organisation, and whether the whole organisation has to change its design, part of the organisation has to change, no design change is required, or whether the change takes place at a structural, system or task level. This scope of change can be described through three levels of work-design changes, as indicated below.

1. The most complex type of design change is when the organisation changes to a new model. In this case, it is likely that the majority of work within the organisation will have to change. To transition to a new model is a major organisation work-design challenge, and normally involves moving to a more complex, higher design. If this happens, the main impact will be on the management and leadership processes in the organisation, which will have to change radically. Some services may be repositioned, and it is possible that processes within value chains may be redefined and reallocated within the organisation.
2. Most organisation work-design initiatives do not change the model but rather redefine the value-generating focus of the organisation. To do this, business units are redefined and work

is distributed differently throughout the organisation through the creation of new income centres or business units. As the value-creating work is redefined, so service and management element work are likely to change. Typical changes are:

- The formation of new business or service units.
- Changing a revenue-generation or cost centre to a business unit.
- The creation of a new division.
- Changing the focus of centralised and decentralised control.
- Changing the focus of work in a business element, for instance from a product-focused design to a customer-focused design.
- Changing the role of the head office.
- Outsourcing or insourcing work.
- Creating synergies by combining business units or creating greater flexibility through making smaller business units.

3. The least complex work-design approach is one where neither the current model nor business elements change.

Minor design changes take place on a regular basis in most organisations to satisfy changing needs of stakeholders and to enable growth efficiencies. These changes, such as changing roles, contracting suppliers, growing into new sales markets and investing in new opportunities, are part of the day-to-day role of managing any organisation.

In all organisations there should be an ongoing challenge as to whether the current volume of work is necessary, as removing work that is not needed will reduce costs and could make the organisation more competitive. However, if these tactical changes do not meet the needs of its stakeholders, then a solution may be a more complex design change.

Complex design change, ie the step up or down to a new model normally occurs over several years through organic growth or in a radical way, for instance as a result of an acquisition or divestment. Complex design change can be regarded as a strategy enabler. For example, a strategy to create a customer-focused organisation could be partly achieved by implementing a customer-centric design.

The context of which organisation is the focus of change is also important, as a small change for the whole organisation could be a transformation for one of its sub-organisations where the majority of that change is taking place.

If a large design process is required for an organisation, then the steps of this process are to define the criteria the design must achieve, review design options and decide on the most suitable design, and then implement the new design. These steps are detailed in the following part of this section.

THE STEPS TO DESIGN AND IMPLEMENT THE MODELS

If a full design process is required, either because it will enable a new strategy or because of a radical change in the organisation such as a merger or acquisition, then the following design process steps should be followed:

STEP 1: THE DEVELOPMENT OF ORGANISATION DESIGN CRITERIA

If a large redesign of work in an organisation has been chosen as a strategic enabler, then it is assumed that the change drivers create a good reason to justify this approach.

The change drivers on an organisation, either from an internal or external perspective, set the context for why an organisation design is required, but they do not clarify what the design needs to achieve or the extent of the change. In order to design an organisation, criteria are needed detailing what the design should achieve. This requires an indepth appreciation of the reasons for the change and what outputs are required by the stakeholders impacted by the change.

Leadership needs to set the design criteria required to align a design to the organisation strategy. These design criteria then form the mandate for design, which is used to evaluate options for designs. The review of options to these criteria will lead to a recommendation for leadership to consider and agree on a design they wish to implement in the organisation.

The accountability of choosing a design lies with the senior leadership team as it is a key enabler of strategy. Many leaders take advice from external experts when designing a large change to understand the pros and cons of the design options available before making a decision.

A work design project team of internal and/or external designers is normally used by the leadership team to collect the information required for the design criteria and review options for designs that they will present as the blueprint report.
The leadership of an organisation must plan for each step change in design in a similar manner to planning other strategic goals. The owner of the design should be the leader in the organisation who

owns the strategy. It is very difficult to separate organisation design from strategy development as the two flow together. The choice of products, markets and internal processes to make an organisation competitive leads directly to decisions about what work is required and what the company needs to look like.

The design team in this analysis phase will review the following:

WHAT ARE THE REASONS FOR AN ORGANISATION DESIGN APPROACH?

It is important to identify the reasons for change and to confirm if they are real or perceived, particularly in terms of internal drivers. This is to ensure that a design process is the optimal option for change in the organisation. In order to appreciate the drivers for change normally, an indepth understanding of the organisation's strategy and the changing needs of the stakeholders is required. At this point, it may be necessary for leadership to meet in order to clarify strategies.

A change in design may be a deliberate leadership decision to reflect a change in strategy and align the activities of the organisation to that strategy. In many cases there is no option but to change the design, such as in a merger or acquisition or when the current design is not supporting the size of the organisation following its growth.

It is important to also question if it is the right time for a new organisation design. Other changes may be required first, such as the implementation of a new IT system or the acquisition of a rival organisation before a new design process is implemented.

WHAT DOES THE PARENT ORGANISATION WANT THE DESIGN TO ACHIEVE?

If the organisation to be designed is part of a larger organisation, then it is important to define the expectations of this parent organisation in terms of the organisation's strategy and design criteria. A design taking place in a sub-organisation of a larger organisation may be restricted in its options due to the design or policies of the larger organisation.

WHAT IS THE CURRENT ORGANISATION DESIGN?

A solid appreciation of the current organisation is required as a starting point from which to build a new design. The current design should be modelled to reflect how the organisation operates. This model should be used as the baseline from which to compare future designs.

Many organisations have grown organically and have no models of how the organisation works. The first step in organisation design is to model the current design.

The simplest step is to categorise the organisation into one of the five types of overall organisation designs. From this categorisation the whole organisation needs to be modelled into the design elements – management structures, business units and service units. The business units or work processes should be categorised into their types, such as geographical, process, or customer. The high-level process in each element should be listed and, if possible, then linked to the number of employees and costs.

If time allows, business and operating models of the current organisation could be of great value but the design team must not lose momentum on moving towards a new design.

The strengths and weaknesses of the current model should be assessed as part of this step.

WHAT ARE THE WORK OUTPUTS EXPECTED FROM THE FUTURE ORGANISATION?

The analysis of the needs of stakeholders as well as change opportunities within the organisation should identify where and by how much the work and processes need to change. This will focus the design on the parts of the organisation requiring change and which parts should be maintained in their current activities.

WHAT ARE THE OPPORTUNITIES TO INCORPORATE BEST PRACTICES INTO A DESIGN?

Although each organisation has its unique characteristics, there tend to be similarities of organisation designs within industries. This similarity of design tends to lead to similar performance. It is worthwhile analysing how innovative competitors or comparable organisations in other industries design their work to assess if a different approach to industry norms would provide a competitive advantage. Benchmarking may, however, also be misleading in organisation design as a solution appropriate to one industry may not be the best solution for another, but it is a good source of ideas.

CREATING DESIGN CRITERIA

The design team at this point will have a good appreciation of the reasons for change and leadership expectations, how work is placed in the current organisation, what its key stakeholder want from the future organisation and what are the opportunities for different designs. This knowledge will then be debated with leadership and used to create a list of design criteria that the new design should achieve.

In reviewing change in the organisation one of the initial decisions will be whether the change required will move the organisation into a different design model. If this is the case then leadership should be aware that the design proposed will impact how they work. A change of design within the same model will be more straightforward than the implementation of a new model.

Leaders might have to make a strategic investment decision to enable growth in an organisation through deciding to implement a higher architectural model earlier than needed to enable the resulting excess leadership resource to develop the organisation to a point where the model is sustainable.

Once the drivers for change and the requirements of outputs have been clarified, then the criteria on which to base the design can be discussed and agreed upon. The design criteria are the outputs expected from a new design and are therefore the performance parameters for measuring the applicability of a proposed design to the needs of the organisation.

The design criteria are a broad expectation of what the design should achieve, and they form the mandate for the design team. As the design enables the strategy, there should be a clear link between the design criteria and the strategic goals of the organisation. The number of criteria required will depend on the complexity of the change: too few will not allow an assessment of the quality of the design and too many may make a design unachievable as they will start to conflict with each other. Normally between five and 20 criteria are applied.

Some examples of design criteria that could be used to support a design are:
- **Minimal central structures:** These would tend to indicate that a small head office is required and work should be decentralised.
- **Increased customer focus:** This could support a move to a more customer-focused design, possibly placing customer-orientated process teams or decentralised sales teams close to their customers.

- **Process-orientated structures:** These could indicate that the current work is split across functions and more multidisciplined process teams are required.
- **Global/regional empowerment:** This would indicate decentralisation of work to the regions away from a central base.
- **Contract out non-core activities:** Investigate options for outsourcing.
- **More business orientation:** A review and redefining of profit units in the organisation.
- **IT enhancements:** Adapt the design to the opportunities created by new IT systems to change the way the organisation works.
- **Technology enhancements:** Fit the design to the opportunities created by new technology to change the way the organisation works.
- **Lean support services:** The current support services need to be refocused and consolidated, possibly with some outsourcing.
- **Cost-effectiveness:** This is to ensure that a design creates greater value than the costs and risks of implementing it.

Note: These criteria are likely to also include direction for the structuring of the organisation, which would follow the design of the elements of the organisation.

For the design criteria chosen, it is useful for the executive to qualify them with acceptable and non-acceptable options for the organisation to provide greater guidance to the design team. If, for example, cost-effectiveness was a criteria it could be qualified by including a target for cost savings and an explanation for the need to reduce the duplication of services in the organisation, but it may also stipulate that outsourcing will not be considered.

The design criteria can be weighted and prioritised against each other in order to get a balanced list of the critical success factors the design needs to achieve. The design criteria should be signed off by the leaders of the organisation as a mandate for what the organisation design team should achieve.

An organisation's leader may sometimes recommend the implementation of a new organisation design model too quickly for the current needs of the organisation. This may be a good investment to enable growth but it may sometimes be recommended as a vanity option. A vanity option is when a leader implements a more complex model than the activities in the organisation require. This is to create a perception that the organisation is successful but it can lead to excess costs and inefficiencies. This could occur when, in a basic management model, a leadership team seems to have been created on paper, which would reflect a more mature unit, but all control is centralised in a single leader who makes all decisions. Other examples are the formation of small business units when teams are needed or when business units are titled divisions to create a perception that the organisation is larger and more complex than it really is.

It is important that the senior managers impacted by the possible changes have their views heard in terms of their perceptions of the changes required. This will help to facilitate ownership of the design criteria and create a need for change in the organisation. The processes for achieving this include one-on-one interviews and workshops between the design team and interested managers.

The design criteria should be supported by clarity on leadership's expectations of the design project. Before design commences, the expectations of the length of the project, the resources to allocate to it, budgets and decision-making governance should all be agreed upon with the programme leaders.

STEP 2: THE DESIGN PHASE

There are myriad options available on how to put together each part of the foundation business model. This makes each business unique with its own culture and performance.

Once the design criteria and overall model have been agreed upon, then the options that could be applied in the organisation need to be considered as the design phase. As an organisation becomes more complex with multiple business units, products and markets, the options for different designs increase.

During the designing phase, most organisations simply copy close competitors. It is the easy approach, and can be visualised by stakeholders. Copying the market should be the safe option, unless the market is changing. However, if the design looks like the competitor, it is likely that the performance it enables will also be similar to that competitor.

Each organisation commences any change in design from the perspective of its own current unique design, which will be influenced by the characteristics of the organisation such as:
- Range of products and markets
- Organisation performance
- Location of operations and markets
- Flexibility of products and services
- Whether they are market leaders or followers
- The complexity of the organisation
- The number of major sub-organisations
- Internationalisation of the organisation
- The growth or contraction of the organisation
- The culture of the organisation
- The views of the leadership team

Not many organisations have the opportunity to create a new organisation design without parameters that dictate at least some of the factors of where work should take place. These include:

- The current physical assets of the organisation, such as factories and offices, are often set as factors that cannot easily be changed. Similarly, an organisation's location (the country or region) also sets some of the parameters of work. For many organisations the location of resources and markets may also impact where the work has to take place.
- The resources available to the organisation, particularly financial, may limit an organisation's choice in how it does work and the options it has to change design.
- The historical work design of an organisation will also set parameters as this provides the base of how work is done in the organisation and any change must be from this base.
- The position of the organisation in its chosen market can impact its choices, such as whether it is a market leader or follower. A market leader often has to do more work than a follower to maintain its leadership position, which the followers copy rather than design for themselves. However, there is no barrier to innovation, and breaking the industry norms through a radical work design can change a follower into a leader.

There are two levels of activity in a design process. The first is to design the elements needed in the organisation so that the overall design framework or architecture is in place. To deliver the design criteria, there could be several feasible options for a design that the leaders could consider. The preferred option for the overall design needs to be agreed upon by leaders before the second stage, which is allocating work from each process in the business into these elements, can take place. In practice high-level assumptions of where work will take place in the organisation are needed to design the elements. When the elements have been designed and work divided accordingly, the leaders of the organisation ought to be able to assess its fit with the design criteria and a final blueprint report written to guide implementation.

DESIGNING THE ELEMENTS

The design process needs to first define the elements where customer value, and therefore profit, is created in the business. In organisations applying the first three models this is only in one business unit and therefore one point of profitability measurement, but in more complex organisations there will be multiple business units. From this core design of the business units, other elements to support this value creation can be added and then work allocated to each element.

Assuming a multiple business unit/company approach is needed, the initial challenge of the design process is to review options and agree how the value-creation work should be split into business unit elements. This challenge involves both the definition of the number of business units, their design orientation and the broad scope of work within each one. This means assessing the pros and cons of each potential option of business unit design compared with the design criteria.

The optimum solution should be one that closely matches the design criteria. The proposals for the business unit design should be approved before further design commences as the rest of the organisation elements support the delivery of values from the business units.

Once the number and focus of the business units have been decided upon, then a decision is needed on whether they need to be clustered into divisions or regional groupings. If clustering is required, the choice will be based on the best grouping option, such as geographical, customer, market or process.

When the business unit elements have been differentiated and their focus agreed upon, the management and support elements can be added. The direct support elements for value-creation activities will be a choice of whether the activities sit in the business units, are centralised in the organisation in service elements, or are outsourced.

In terms of the management elements of the structure and their related management and strategic services, the organisation's business philosophy of centralisation/decentralisation and standardisation/bureaucracy needs to be questioned to identify where this work should take place. From this assessment and taking into account the number and differences of focus between business units, regional, divisional and head office, splits of work can be designed. As these designs take place there are normally revisions to the other elements to ensure synergy and a balanced model.

It is at this point that options of moving work in or out of the organisation should be considered. These options to in- or outsource work will impact the size and number of elements the business requires.

A final element in the design is to assess whether any transition elements are needed in the design, such as project units, which may be needed for a period of time but are not permanent features of the organisation. A large design implementation is often supported by projects to change systems and processes.

The decisions on business units, service units and leadership teams allow an organisation picture of its major elements to be produced, similar to the one below, which was discussed earlier.

Different Elements in Organisation Design

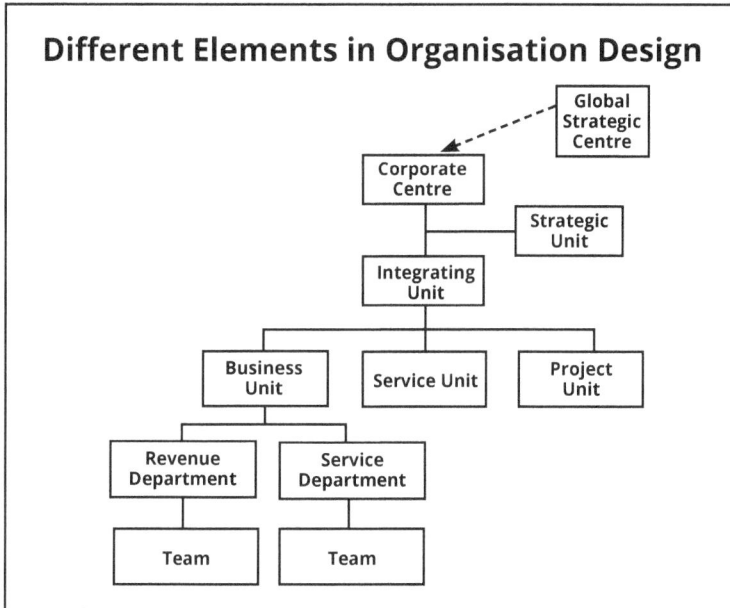

In the process of design there are probably several design options for leadership to consider, each with their own pros and cons. Debate on the design options should be carefully managed as options can cause uncertainty in the organisation. A small team of leaders should debate options and quickly discard any unsuitable ones to limit the risk that they are leaked to a wider audience. Leadership needs to balance the needs of making one of the most important choices for the organisation's long-term success with the internal organisation's expectation of clarity of direction.

Once leadership approval is gained for an option, more detail needs to be added to allocate work to each element.

ALLOCATING WORK TO THE BUSINESS ELEMENTS

It is a choice of leadership where work should be done in the organisation and how it should be done. In order to do this we need to consider two major concepts: firstly, deciding how work should be done in the organisation, which is a factor of its culture, centralisation philosophy and chosen work processes; and secondly, how to split this work up to the different elements. The output of this is to allocate the work needed in the organisation to its different parts.

The starting point for splitting the work up is an agreement of the work required in the organisation with the chosen technical processes and an agreement of the major elements in the business.

In most cases there is a natural split of work into elements and it is likely that only 10% of the work processes will be under debate as to where they should be placed in an organisation. Sometimes this process will lead to the reassessment of some of the design elements and so it is often done in parallel with the design of the elements.

In general terms, some rules to follow for where to place the work in the organisation are as follows:
  • If work is dedicated to an element, it should be placed in that element.
  • If work is across a number of elements, then it should be in a service unit or management structure.
  • If the work is not full time, it should be considered for a service element or outsourcing.
  • If work is strategic and/or core for competitiveness, it should be maintained in the business.

In order to commence this approach, the work processes in the organisation need to be listed at a high level of detail and then the sub-processes within these large processes defined in more detail. The amount of detail required needs only to be enough to split up the work into the different elements of the business. The fine detail of defining the work down to individual roles and positions is part of structuring.

Some typical high-level activities in an organisation could be:
- Creation of product or service
- Financial management
- Human resource management
- Planning
- Customer service
- Raw materials
- Delivery of services
- IT infrastructure
- Quality management
- Safety
- Equipment maintenance

Each of these high-level activities should be broken down into processes, which may need to be split further into sub-processes for the effective allocation of the work. The list required will depend on the processes in each organisation and the choices made in the organisation of what work it wants to do. Sometimes, particularly for management processes, it is beneficial to define the focus of activities as an output that the stakeholders want rather than an internal process like human resource management. This can add a new dimension to the process and allows the leaders to see the organisation differently. Some examples of this type of activity may include:
- Making money
- Asset management
- Corporate governance
- Future direction
- Knowledge management
- Optimisation of employee potential

Each process requiring change in the organisation needs to be mapped and the work allocated to an element in the organisation. When a large aspect of an organisation, such as finance, is reviewed, the processes within this aspect need to be split into three levels of focus. The first level is the activities that are part of the value chain that create value for the organisation. The second level is activities that can be termed operational support processes – these exist because of the value chain and therefore support the value-chain process. The third level is strategic processes, which direct the future of the organisation and would be largely unchanged even if the value chain radically changed.

Splitting the processes into strategic, operational support and value chain enables the work required in an organisation to be allocated to different parts of the organisation. Most value-chain activities take place in profit/service delivery business units. Operational support processes are either within business units, or are supplied to all business units in some kind of project or shared service structure, and strategic processes normally reside in the head office, division or group strategic centre structures. This process of allocating work is shown in the model below:

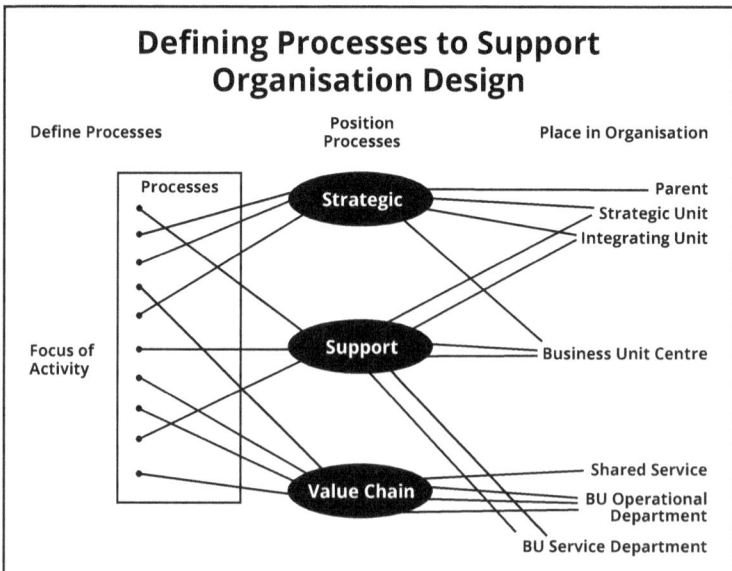

Defining Processes to Support Organisation Design

The quantity of work to be completed also needs to be defined. The amount of work may be too much for a single element, therefore more elements need to be designed. Or there may be enough work to enable elements such as service units, which in turn achieve economies of scale. The type of work will dictate how the quantity of work is measured, for example, man hours, unit volumes and machine hours. This quantification of work should take place at a high enough level for it to be split. At this point it is not an issue of how many people or machines will be required to do the work as this is part of the structure and infrastructure design.

It is at this point in the design when current ways of working in the organisation can be challenged. The new organisation design should enable long-term competitiveness, which will only be achieved if the processes within it are competitive. Although the majority of the high-level activities in the organisation will not change, the design team should challenge the processes within each activity and recommend any changes to inefficient systems. Understanding which processes are changing and where they fit in the organisation will lead to further clarity of where change is needed in the organisation.

The extent of this process change will influence the challenge of the new organisation design. Moving to a new design may involve substantial changes to the work in an organisation leading to a new people structure, leadership team changes, new IT systems, revised procedures, new technology and new policies. Actualising a vision of a dramatically changed organisation can take several years to achieve.

The main reason why the commencement of a new organisation design should not be taken lightly is the knock-on effect it has on all other areas of the organisation. It changes what may initially have been seen as a small project into a transformation programme, which the organisation needs to be prepared for if it is to be achieved effectively.

These pictures of the organisation need to be supported by a blueprint report that describes how the organisation works and details the work done in different elements of the organisation.

A BLUEPRINT OF THE DESIGN

In order to provide the leadership team with the information they require to make a decision on whether the design meets their needs and will deliver their strategy, a blueprint report should be produced by the design team that details all the information necessary to make a decision, including options for design.

Most blueprint reports will be straightforward, but a more global focus on world trade has opened up more options for where work takes place if the organisation has the financial resources to gain this flexibility. In this world, blueprint scenarios and options can be very complex.

Organisations can now manufacture in different countries to their markets and even outsource some of their service needs internationally, such as the trend for call centres to India. This globalisation has provided greater flexibility in the options for work design and the choices a large organisation has for how to deliver its work.

When an organisation design is proposed by the project team, it should be reviewed against its alignment to the design criteria to measure its suitability. The design criteria are therefore the performance measures for the work design process.

A checklist of questions for leadership to ask in order to assess if the design is appropriate could be:
- Does it meet the majority of the design criteria mandated?
- Does it reflect the work required for the strategy of the organisation?
- Will the work required by external stakeholders be satisfied?

- Will the cost of implementing this design justify its benefits?
- Will the impact of implementing this design and the disruption to the organisation be within the acceptable risk appetite?
- Is the design flexible enough to cope with possible market scenarios?
- Will the design stand up to current competition and any possible competitive threats in the future?
- Does the design match the technology and work processes used in the organisation?
- Will the design be able to gain the critical mass of support from stakeholder and especially employee groups to support its implementation.

In deciding on a design, the following implications need to be considered by leadership:

- Each option will have its own pros and cons. Leadership needs to consider how to maximise the pros and minimise the cons. This may mean that new information systems will be required to define pictures of the business, which will not be shown in the design.
- Leadership needs to consider the impact on policies, procedures and work practices that will need to change, particularly with regards to their roles in the organisation as they will be the sponsors of change.
- The culture of the organisation that will support this design and how this will differ from the current culture.
- The groups of stakeholders who will be most impacted by the changes and their possible reactions to these changes. Mobilising approaches will be needed to support change with these stakeholders.
- The time, resources and costs to implement the changes. The cost of the design may be too much for the organisation and a simpler design may need to be considered. The cost needs to consider the disruption to working practices created by the design and the possible impact on performance. In terms of timing, sometimes a

design needs to be implemented in phases as the overall change would put too much pressure on the organisation if attempted in one go.
- What will be the impact be on current employees and how are they likely to react to the design? Is the design going to need more or less employees and will the employees be different to current employees in terms of competencies?
- How to communicate the new design to stakeholders so that they understand the reasons for change and support the new design.

After considering these implications, questions and the alignment of the design to the set design criteria, a decision needs to be made by the leadership on the option to implement. This decision should be shown as a sign-off of the work design blueprint report (with agreed changes), which can be used as the mandate for implementing the change in the organisation.

If an organisational work design process has been completed successfully, then there should be at least the following outputs detailed in the final blueprint report:

- A picture of how the organisation currently works.
- Criteria for the outputs of a new organisation work design.
- The macro model of the whole new organisation.
- The focus and links between the business elements in the organisation to show how work should flow.
- A description of the work that needs to be conducted within each element, and the expected high-level outputs.
- A description detailing the changes required and how the organisation should work in the future (this will be the major input into the structuring process).
- Implementation plans including action plans and timeframes.
- A communication process for the design.

The choice of model decided upon for the organisation work design will have pros and cons. The cons of the model will normally be that alternative ways of looking at the business have not been chosen and so there may be gaps in how the organisation sees itself. Information pictures are needed to reflect hidden processes in the organisation, allowing leadership to make decisions on all aspects of the performance of the organisation and its processes.

It is important for leaders in an organisation to understand the benefits of the chosen design but also to ensure that they can view the organisation from a variety of perspectives. So an organisation that has chosen to split its business units by geographical elements may want to invest in great customer segmentation information systems and financial systems that show profitability by product. Although the geographical model may have been optimal for management, other pictures of the organisation are required to enhance an understanding of the organisation to support great decision-making. These new pictures will not be organisation designs but information-driven and linked to the organisation's systems.

STEP 3: IMPLEMENTATION

Implementation is the process of changing the organisation to the agreed blueprint design. This can be a quick process involving leadership informing the organisation that a simple change is taking place through to a programme of change lasting several years. The options for implementation are huge if we consider work design changes in all organisations. Without going into the detail of how to manage change projects, the following implementation approaches and challenges will be found in each model.

The initial implementation of an organisation work design is when it is first formed, with the business intent being turned into the activities of a foundation business model. As mentioned earlier, a new organisation can be formed at any of the model complexities, with the challenges increasing as the model complexity increases but, in this example, we will assume that the new organisation is a start-up model.

Initiating a start–up model requires the owners or allocated leaders to have a clear idea of how they want to start the organisation and put the first building blocks in place. This means that for each box of the foundation model, an asset or activity is put in place. Premises are found, first employees recruited, machines installed, and products produced and sold. The leader must be able to clearly articulate the business intent and plans to attract resources, including employees and create customer interest in the product or service.

In a start-up model the work design and implementation of the value chains and the work to meet legislation are the key activities of the leaders of the organisation and it will take up a substantial amount of the leader's time until the processes are running smoothly.

Most start-up organisations are copies of other similar organisations such as shops, farms, professional services, schools, restaurants, charities and construction companies. How these teams work is fairly standard in a market with clear regulations and a wide variety of external services in place to support this new activity. The challenge for the start-up is to break into the market by quickly attracting and retaining a customer base. In these organisations, the work design focus will be on creating the team to deliver the products or services that differentiate the organisation from competitors. Many of these organisations will not change this initial design format.

For other organisations the start-up model is seen as just the initial stepping stone to quickly grow to a more complex model. In this case again each box of the foundation model needs to be filled but with an eye on what further change will be required soon so that this first investment provides longer-term value. The leader(s) or entrepreneur(s) should spend time thinking about how work and roles will change as the organisation grows. The earlier clarity on the expected roles of each of the key members of the organisation is defined, the easier the transition to the basic management model will be.

Implementing the basic management model is a straightforward organisational change, involving moving one or more roles into dedicated management above the value-chain team. It is not a complex change, rather a gradual one as the work outside of the value chain grows with the organisation and the leader finds they are doing less and less direct value-creation activities.

The organisation will still be small in this model and the challenge will be around personalities and the agreement of where the decision-making powers lie. Getting the right people for management, sales and product or service delivery roles will be key to the ongoing maturing of the organisation.

A business unit will gradually grow to the mature model, with value-chain production and sales being the key drivers of this growth. Continual work design adaptations will be needed to tweak the organisation during incremental growth stages. At some point the organisation will grow to a stage where the leadership team will not know everything going on in the organisation by simply asking questions, walking around and basic monitoring of performance. This creates the need for the first significant work design implementation to formalise activities in the organisation.

This is the challenge of managing the organisation through information, policy and meeting structures. It can be seen as centralising control and creating bureaucracy. Much of this process will consist of gradual changes but some larger initiatives are likely to be tackled as projects. Some of the projects will be to install functional IT systems and processes so that work can in insourced from previous suppliers to growing functional teams.

As a business unit matures, the volume of work increases and it has more options on how to complete this work in a manner that is competitive. There are more options as to which markets to enter, what products to sell, locations for activities, and the employment of more people in structures.

The implementation of change becomes more challenging as locations increase and more value chains are needed. This creates a need for more design elements to be implemented in the form of income and service units. Splitting work from one element into several will require careful design. Work needs to be allocated between value-chain and support services, and between value-creation department supervisors, middle management and senior leadership. This will require more management information as many roles will be more remote from the activity, and work will become split across functional teams.

For most mature business unit organisations, these changes and implementations are part of managing a business and organisation design aspects of projects are a small part of activities to improve the organisation.

Work design and implementation are a big challenge for the corporate model. It is a step change from the challenges of design in a mature business unit. There are many more options for designs, and implementation of large changes is extremely complex. Programmes of change can require hundreds of team members and take years to fully implement. In this complexity of organisation most large change programmes have an element of work redesign and restructuring of roles. To manage this change requires a range of competencies, such as programme management and project teams.

Creating a global strategic centre above corporate model organisations is not normally a large implementation. The challenge is to design how it will operate and what work it will do – this is where the investment in time should be placed. The challenge of the model is to create more value from the group for investors than if they individually invested in corporate model organisations. The core of this centre is normally an executive board with a few specialist supportive roles to ensure governance and strategic direction. Getting this model right is all about individuals in the team who can come together to unlock value from the organisations in the group.

Once the overall design has been agreed upon, selling the concept and implementation processes to the rest of the organisation should begin.

Most designs will have been developed and agreed upon by a few senior leaders and specialist advisors. If the strategy is clear and the strengths and weaknesses of the main elements of the organisation well known, then the design process should be completed in days or weeks, after which it needs to be sold to a wider leadership team and key stakeholders.

The main communication tool with which leadership sells the new design to an organisation will be the blueprint. This can be summarised at different levels of detail depending on the audience. The blueprint is used to gain buy-in for the new design, to explain the reasons for change and to be a guide for more detailed design.

The organisation's leaders need to be prepared for the following questions from key stakeholders:

- How does this design support the achievement of the strategy?
- Why is this change necessary?
- What investment will be needed?
- How long will it take to implement?
- What other options were considered?
- How does it impact my role? (Pertinent to senior executives.)
- What is the process to split up work and restructure roles?

The choices made in the design are likely to lead to winners and losers in the organisation's leadership team, and it should become evident fairly quickly how much support there is for the design. If a significant number of stakeholders reject the design or the reaction is a negative one, this could either be the result of a poor design process or possibly a poor communication process.

If there is a perception that it is a poor design, it will need to be addressed urgently. This may involve noting the concerns, reviewing whether they are valid, and if they were omitted by the design team. If this is the case, the design needs to be changed in consideration of this feedback; if not, it may lead to a lack of understanding of the reasons for change and an improved communication drive will be required. If the design is weak and it will not achieve the organisation's desired strategy for reasons missed in the design phase but now identified by stakeholders, it should also be changed. With any design there will be consequences. A downsizing design could result in many redundancies; other designs impacting senior individuals will need a judgement taken on whether to win over initial detractors to the design or to let them leave the organisation and replace them with supporters.

At this stage of the organisation's change processes, leadership is needed in the main elements of the design so that they can own the next phase of the design, which is resourcing the elements to deliver the organisation's work and strategy. It should be remembered that these models are for the whole organisation. If elements within the organisation need to change their work then a similar design process will be needed for each element.

Drawing the picture, writing the blueprint and having it agreed upon are the easy parts of the process. Changing where and how work is delivered has a knock-on effect to many aspects of how the organisation is operated. Numerous changes will be needed: from realigning IT systems to allocating new cost centres. In initiating a new design process, leaders need to be aware that the change could impact nearly every aspect of their business – from causing disruptions to sourcing investment for the implementation. An immediate impact of choosing a new work design will be on employees' roles.

When communicating the reasons for a new organisation model, it is natural for the reviewing staff to question how the design impacts them and their current roles. The design model itself does not answer this question and to implement the design, a people structure to support it is required. This structure design will define each role in the organisation and for each role a competent employee is required.

Even in the simplest redesign, at least a few employees will change roles and then changes to policies, processes and procedures will be needed to align to the new allocation of work. An organisation design must describe the organisation in appropriate detail to implement this. The type of detail that could be required may be the number and location of branches, the number of machines required, and how many products will be produced. To allow the right number of people to be structured, the roles and positions have to be defined and then they can be resourced with competent employees, equipment and new systems.

The design model does not reflect the complexity of the work involved – the work a team performs in these models may be very simple, such as repetitively packing boxes or extremely complex, such as inventing a new drug. However, this complexity is extremely important in structuring competent people into roles within this design. In a start-up business, the work can either be very simple such as subsistence farming or highly complex such as IT. As the models become more complex, work becomes more defined and minimum levels of capability are required to deal with the complexity of leading a complex organisation. The complexity of an organisation design does lead to some broad assumptions on work complexity. To manage a multidisciplined leadership team in a mature business unit requires general management competencies across all these disciplines and to effectively chair the board of a global enterprise will require a highly complex range of business competencies.

With a new people structure, there will be a need in most designs to change many other aspects of the organisation to align to the new design. Policies, processes and information flow are likely to change, as well as the governance forums, particularly if the design changes up or down to a new model. These changes will be needed to ensure that work flows in the manner designed. Policies and procedures will need to be written to define how the business should operate within the new design. Frequently, a new design requires a significant IT investment to align systems to the new philosophies.

If the number of stakeholders leads to the choice of the most appropriate model, the sum of the work required from these stakeholders in terms of tasks leading to measured outputs will dictate the processes and people structures within an organisation.

The organisation design is a strategic tool picturing how the organisation should work, but in itself it will have made no change to the organisation as it is not installed until people have been structured and inducted into the work demanded from the design.

Work has to be delivered through people or machines, both of which must be competent to deliver the required work. The key enabler to the implementation of the design is therefore the organisational structure and the placement of competent individuals for each required role.

The models in this book are broad, and although each organisation will have its own unique aspects of the design, competitors can copy the majority of a design's features. Therefore the effective structuring of the right people in an organisation can be viewed as an organisation's only long-term competitive advantage.

If the design process has been successful, then its conclusion should be senior leadership and stakeholder support for the design and an agreement that this is the optimum approach to deliver the organisation's strategy.

SUMMARY

An organisation design aims to deliver the work an organisation chooses to do within its chosen processes. If the organisation has chosen to do the wrong work to achieve its strategy or the processes chosen are not competitive, the organisation design will not overcome these fundamental problems. The design of what work to do and the strategy to achieve it underpins the organisation design.

The design of where work should take place in an organisation can take anything from a couple of hours in a simple organisation to six months or more in the most complex organisations. The project delivery requirements would be vastly different for each of these scenarios, so this section has focused on the more complex change process.

An agreement of the design criteria leads to an analysis of design options and eventually choosing one or more designs to present to leadership for discussion and approval. With leadership support the design can move into implementation.

An organisation design should produce the following outputs on its completion:
- Clarity of relationships with external stakeholders of the organisation.
- Defined centralised and decentralised activities.
- The location of value-chain processes and their expected outputs.
- The location of management processes and their expected outputs.
- Clarity of profit and cost centres in the organisation.
- Interpreting management philosophies into how the organisation should work – this will lead to the desired culture.
- An appreciation of the different levels of leadership required in the organisation.

In larger change processes, these outputs should be detailed in a design blueprint.

If where work is placed in the organisation changes, there will be a knock-on impact that involves changing many of the processes used to manage current work. A new work design will lead directly into the design of new structures and processes and it will not be fully implemented until these role structures and aligned processes have also been implemented

With all these implementation challenges and their associated costs and risks, is it worthwhile changing an organisation's design? The conclusion that follows addresses whether the design is either part of the long-term success or failure of the organisation.

SUCCESS AND FAILURE IN ORGANISATION DESIGNS

How do you measure the success of an organisation design?

The most conclusive test is the longevity of a design. Military hierarchies, religious organisations, such as the Catholic Church, and government approaches are some of the best examples of designs of complex organisations that have stood the test of time.

An organisation can survive for hundreds if not thousands of years. One of the earliest continuous organisations is the Chengdu Shishi Middle School in China founded between 143 and 141 BC. Other good examples of smaller organisation designs that have stood the test of time include those retail businesses whose core format would have changed little from their earliest beginnings, such as butchers and bakers.

According to a report published by the Bank of Korea in May 2008, in which 41 countries were analysed, there were 5 586 companies older than 200 years. Of these 3 146 are located in Japan, 837 in Germany, 222 in the Netherlands and 196 in France. 89.4% of the companies with more than 100 years of history are businesses employing less than 300 people. A nationwide Japanese survey counted more than 21 000 companies older than 100 years as at 30 September 2009.

Waiting for hindsight on the longevity of a design is not helpful to leaders trying to optimise their current organisation. Leaders have to either assess the design performance of similar organisations in the market or have a good intuitive feel that the approach they propose will work. In assessing other organisations, the measures of the design will be linked to the organisation's performance. This approach assumes that there is a direct link between a design and performance. Some of these measures are:
- Achieving the current design model
- Size of market share

- Brand recognition
- Number of employees
- Profitability – although rapidly growing organisations may not focus on this, preferring to invest
- Capital value
- Share value – a good measure of expectations of future performance

It is unlikely that all these criteria will be met and it could be argued that other factors are behind the performance, such as a great product, a strong brand or innovative technology. An organisation can only choose one design at a time so it is difficult to compare performance to what it would have been like with a different design. Benchmarking performance to internal peer and external competitor organisations applying different designs can indicate whether the design applied in an organisation is appropriate. However, benchmarking is difficult as there are many factors that influence performance. The design models in this book can aid this analysis as the best benchmarks will be to peers and competitors applying the same model. Organisations need to also be aware of direct competitors applying a different model and allocation of work, as these may be the ones that are breaking the traditional rules in the market.

Organisations have found that creating a new paradigm of how work could be done can have huge strategic advantages. Often the full benefit of organisation design is to break the rules. Following tried-and-tested approaches may provide incremental improvements but a radical shift could capture a new, larger section of the market.

The most dramatic designs are the ones that break an industry paradigm, such as Ford's production line on car manufacture or Amazon's impact on bookshops. When a new model becomes the norm in an industry and the old way of working declines, the design can be classed as truly successful.

Most organisations never make it to global organisation level. However, organisations in each model can be classed as successful because growth is not always the best measure.

Failure is normally reflected using the same measures. Failure can be the slow stagnation of the business, or a much worse performance as compared with competitors in a similar industry. This could mean the organisation is forced to revert to a lower complexity design. A poor design will always lead to performance problems.

If the organisation's design is inappropriate for the organisation and its desired strategy, it is probable that some of the following problems will be observed in the organisation.
- Inadequate management information leading to poor organisation performance management.
- A poor delivery of internal services to the value-creating elements of the organisation.
- A lack of flexibility to stakeholder change, leading to a slow response to new expectations.
- Inappropriate structure and placement of competencies into roles.
- Internal competition between different elements of the organisation, creating barriers to improved performance.
- Poor flows of information leading to slow decision-making.

These problems will lead to higher costs, lower levels of performance and a lack of competitiveness. Eventually, if there is no improvement, smaller organisations will close and their assets sold. Larger organisations that fail are normally acquired or merge with competitors in a forced process and their independent identity is lost or taken over by new owners.

If an organisation fails, its design will only be one of the factors in this failure as it is only one factor in success. Organisations of all sizes also fail for many reasons that are not related to their designs, such as recessions, lack of funding, poor management, more effective competitors or changing customer demands.

However, some of the reasons for failure are specific to the design of each of the models, outlined as follows:

START-UP

Start-ups are particularly vulnerable to failure. In the first year of existence, up to 25% will fail and probably half will not survive four years. For many the business or organisation intent idea is really not that great, meaning that the market for the product or service is not as good as the entrepreneur envisaged.

From an internal perspective the small size of these organisations normally means they do not have a large pool of resources to get the organisation through difficult times. If scarce skills are lost, key employees become sick or the investment money runs out, the organisation may be forced to close.

The majority of failures in these small organisations are down to leadership incompetence or a lack of experience. Some of the common factors for failure are:

- Opening in the wrong place at the wrong time
- Lack of planning
- Poor pricing decisions
- The volume of business does not justify the costs
- Income falls because of competition
- Lack of competency in the team to deliver the service for customers
- Trying to grow too quickly

This model is all about the abilities of the small team. It is particularly important that the people owning the initiative, either emotionally (as it is their idea) or financially, need to have the energy and enthusiasm to grow the business to at least the next model and make it successful. As there is no structured organisation design, only a team, the team members have to cooperate effectively to deliver the outputs the stakeholders need.

One of the key challenges of this model is time. In this team it is likely that only a small percentage of staff has the inclination and drive to grow the business. These individuals are likely to be the entrepreneurs who started the venture but they have to be involved in creating value for customers and day-to-day management activities leaving little time for growing the business. If time cannot be found for the activities to grow the organisation, it will remain a start-up and the potential of the business idea could be diminished.

BASIC MANAGEMENT

In the growth to a basic management design, success in terms of organisation design lies in the transition to a team that includes a formal leadership role. The choice of leader and their positioning as a role apart from the team creates a climate where there is a risk of the team splitting up due to individual rivalries. It is probably an easier transition if the leadership role is filled by the entrepreneur who started the company as this is normally the person who had to take many of the decisions within the start-up team. The choice becomes more complex if more than one entrepreneur initiated the start-up. The person who had the great start-up idea or provided the financial investment is not always the best person to lead this next stage of growth or even the person who wants this fulltime leadership role. The person who is chosen to lead this stage of organisation growth must make decisions that some members of the team may disagree with. The biggest risk with this transition is that the team splits due to unhappiness with the choice and views of the new leader.

This could just be a hiccup in the growth if team members who leave are quickly replaced but if the split is more serious the design may revert back to a start-up model or the organisation may fail and close.

MATURE BUSINESS

In a mature model the organisation should have proved the viability of its business intent so, unless the market changes, the success or failure of this model is largely dependent on the way the teams in the organisation work together.

The leader or leaders in a basic management model frequently keep in touch with everything going on in the business on a day-to-day basis. This knowledge of what is happening in the business becomes more difficult as the organisation grows. Too much activity is happening in this model for the leaders to be personally aware of each activity so they have to rely on a flow of information to manage the business. This information needs to be summarised at each level of the organisation so that appropriate decisions can be made and all aspects of performance measured.

One of the critical needs of an organisation as it grows is to maintain an understanding of where and how it delivers a margin over costs. It is easy to lose a view of profitability as work is split up across multiple teams, some delivering income and others creating costs.

In this model there will be team-leader and middle-management roles, possibly in several hierarchy levels. These roles link value-creating roles to the most senior leaders and create a new need for internal work to manage managers. This creates the need for procedures, policy meetings and, particularly, management information.

Management information is needed because face-to-face communication is no longer effective due to the size of the organisation and leadership requires pictures of how the organisation is performing to support decision-making. These pictures are found in all functions such as profit and loss accounts in finance, production volumes in a factory, and customer sales from marketing. Many organisations fail because their information systems do not support the control of performance and effective decision-making.

Information needs to flow across the business to deliver the value chain but many functional departments work in silos from the rest of the organisation, forcing information up the hierarchy before it can cross to another silo. This slow information flow is a risk for this model as it potentially makes the organisation hard to manage and slow to change. An effective information system is key to the success of this model and failure is often the result of leaders not appreciating what is really happening in the organisation.

In an organisation with a strong functional silo approach, there is a risk of 'empire building' where the functional teams expand to grow their political strength within the business without any clear link to the benefits for the overall business. An organisation like this will have excess costs that will negatively impact its performance.

The splitting up of work across the teams becomes more important for competitive success as the quantity and variety of this work increases. The choice of where to place work in the organisation is mainly governed by which function it falls into but within this, work is then split further into functional or process teams. How work is grouped into team delivery is critical for this model. If the work is not split effectively the teams will be inefficient, leading to the risk that stakeholders will not be satisfied. If customer stakeholders are not satisfied they will move to competitors and the business will risk failure.

205

The model is a single complex business unit, which means it has a single point of profit accountability with the most senior leader. This means that one of the key challenges for this model, especially if the business has grown rapidly, is to ensure that its most senior leader has the experience and knowledge to manage effectively across all functions. In less complex business units the leader is often an expert in the core business of the organisation with some knowledge of other aspects of business. This means that the leader of a basic management may not be the best person to be the general manager of a more complex business. If the leader does not have multifunctional experience, it is likely that the management of the business will overemphasise the functions they are strong in and long-term plans will not be balanced across all functions.

Best practices need to be encouraged in the functions as it is likely that many competitors will have similar business models and technical processes. A key challenge for the organisation will be to attract employees who can bring functional best practices into the organisation to create a competitive organisation in the current market and maintain competitiveness as the external environment changes. These roles are likely to be the heads of the function, possibly some of the more senior team leaders and individual technical expert roles. An organisation that does not keep up with the times and relies on out-of-date practices opens up its market to competitors applying more up-to-date practices.

Although more activities will be needed internally to deliver the increasing quantity of work, being cost-effective compared with competitors is vital for this design and the mix of insourcing and outsourcing services will be an important factor for this. Internal systems will need to become more standardised in this model and there will be more need for functional systems. The challenge for the organisation is to ensure that these systems support best practices and do not create bureaucracy in the organisation that will increase costs.

Being successful in this model brings the risk that the organisation grows so large that the leadership cannot focus on both the shorter-term operational issues to deliver profit and the longer-term strategic issues to develop the organisation for growth. Normally if this happens the strategic aspects of the role are dropped as the short-term issues take up an increasing volume of leadership work, which is a cycle that only gets worse as longer-term solutions to solve problems are not implemented.

CORPORATE

This model should be more effective than a mature business unit model in managing profitability in a complex business and developing strategy over a longer term such as five to 10 years.

In this complexity of business a good organisation design has the greatest impact on competitiveness and performance but conversely it is also a model with the greatest risk – getting it wrong could lead to the failure of the organisation.

A large organisation utilising the corporate model multiplies all the potential risks of the mature business unit. The problems linked to splitting up work between teams in the business unit model are now magnified as work is divided between business units, service units and suppliers. Mitigation of these risks in a large organisation is that a failure of one business unit may have a limited impact on the performance of the whole organisation.

It is up to the organisation how many business units it will have, what work each will do, how much to invest in each and where they will be located. The choice of organisation design is not often the only factor for the failure of an organisation; the choices of products, prices, markets and technology all play a part. But an organisation can influence all these factors especially with regards the choice of the focus of work in the unit such as customers, which technology process to use and the choice of geographical locations.

Similar choices of the positioning of service units and suppliers outside of the business units are needed for the corporate model. The effectiveness of these services will have an impact on cost competitiveness. In this size of organisation there is a constant challenge to maintain the balance between centralised and decentralised control and this will ebb and flow as the organisation grows and its environment changes. Pulling activities into centralised service units creates control and economies of scale, but it can lead to a reduced ability of business unit leadership teams to manage their profitability, and if the centralisation goes too far they revert to income centres with profitability decisions having to be made by the central leadership team.

Failure of the chosen design for this model is normally a drawn-out process, typified by the organisation's poor performance compared with competitor peers. Just as a successful strategy at this level of organisation complex may take five to 10 years to show its full potential, a poor strategy often takes a similar time period to show its full negative impact on the business.

Organisations that grow to this complexity have previously been successful in less complex models and so there should be a reserve of capital and assets that will be depleted by a poor design but may also hide some of the immediate problems. If a design is weak, some of the symptoms in the performance of the organisation may be:

- Rising costs to income produced
- Targets not being achieved
- Slow delivery of change projects
- Competitors leading in the introduction of new technologies or products
- Declining customer satisfaction in the organisation's products and services
- Increasing staff turnover

An assumption in a successful corporate model is that the leadership in the corporate centre are a step-up, in their capability and capacity, on the individual business unit leaders. They need this capability to align the organisation to the changing demands of the external environment and position the whole organisation for long-term success. Without this step-up in capability, centralised leaders will try to keep the complex business running like a mature business unit. This is likely to result in too little control in business units, so they are sales-focused income centres rather than profit centres. This results in huge pressure on the central team to manage profitability and strategic direction, frequently leading to the poor performance of both activities.

The executive leadership team of this model of design is normally made up of the CEO and then the heads of the divisions and larger business units and senior functional leaders, such as the financial director. When this team meets to lead the organisation, each member must appreciate the multifunctional challenges facing the organisation and should not just represent their functional silo in decision-making. If the leadership team maintains a functional silo view rather than a multifunctional view of the whole corporate organisation, too much pressure will be put onto the CEO as the only multifunctional role in the centre to make all decisions impacting on profitability. If the leadership team does not appreciate the strategic nature of its role, then capital will be poorly allocated, costs will not be optimised, synergies will be lost and there will not be a competitive five-year strategy designed for the organisation.

An essential aspect of implementing this model is creating an effective corporate office with a strategic focus that is not being pulled down into trying to manage the units. Smaller organisations normally buy in specialist strategic advice but the corporate models are big enough to employ specialists on strategic issues that can provide a competitive advantage due to their dedicated focus on the issues impacting the organisation. An effective centralised team ought to protect the corporate organisation from one of the most common reasons for failure of this model, ie being slow to change when the external environment and or market changes. These organisations normally have to ride industry-wide trends, but when the industry itself changes, the organisation that can lead or quickly adapt to these changes will be the most successful.

It is easy to make this level of design too complex with too many business and service units. Being too complex will lead to higher costs and it will be complex to manage with more hierarchies of management and a risk of high levels of bureaucracy that need to control it. However, the complexity of the organisation design needs to reflect the complexity of its environment. Failure sometimes occurs when an organisation design, which works in one location or country, is duplicated in another without consideration of the environment. Materials supply, outsourcing opportunities, weather, the skills of the workforce and utility supply are just some of the factors that can influence the required design of an organisation, and which can change with each location.

As the design failures become more obvious in the market, some of the symptoms could be declining share prices, reduced market share and difficulty in attracting scarce competencies. Failure of this level of organisation means some form of divestment of assets – this could be that the whole business or only part of it is sold. If it is not sold, failure leads to the organisation design reverting to a mature business model.

A stage of failure of the corporate model will probably occur due to too many units reporting to a central leadership function, leading poor control from the centre. This problem can be initially relieved through the implementation of divisional or regional design elements. These will relieve the operational pressure on the centre and allow it to direct the organisation more strategically.

GLOBAL

The global model has its foundation in the belief that the influence of the global centre can create synergies for investors. The investors will expect the portfolio to deliver greater returns than the sum of the estimated returns if each organisation in the group were independent. Therefore a sign of failure for this model will be based on poor returns to the shareholders of the global organisation. The global team positioned centrally above the corporate model organisations should provide this value. If these leaders and the processes they apply are not effective in creating value, then this model will have been seen to fail. However, investors will face a challenge in measuring this performance as the impact of many decisions will take several years to show their potential for success or failure.

As there is no larger model, this is the ultimate design. Further success is measured in continued growth in size, influence and profitability of the portfolio. As the organisations are extremely large and decisions by this top band of leaders will take many years even decades to show their value, success is therefore often only seen in hindsight. The size and influence of these global organisations normally mean that their leaders are well known to the broader public and their views influence the industries they specialise in. Therefore the key factor for success could be the genius of the top leaders to accurately predict the future and turn this into effective decisions.

The key factors for success of this model are likely to be:
- The organic growth of a great idea leaders have invested in.
- The wisdom of leaders whose insight into chosen markets has been recognised by industry leaders.
- The growth of capital strength in the central organisation.
- Capital gain of listed shareholding.
- A great internal culture within the organisation.
- Public support from external stakeholders.
- Brand strength with high levels of customer satisfaction.
- The positioning of great leaders in corporate structures.
- Proven success in knowing when to invest in or sell shareholding.

Failure for this size of organisation, and the leaders within it, is when it is forced to sell assets at the wrong time to optimise capital returns. When this happens, the organisation becomes weaker; it may downsize to a corporate model organisation or even dissolve.

The frequent reasons for failure, some of which are also common to smaller models, are:
- Poor due diligence for mergers and acquisition, leading to poor investment decisions.
- The economic conditions are not accurately forecast by the leaders and so these conditions reduce the anticipated returns.

- An emotional attachment by leaders to the wrong market.
- There is a major disaster in part of the organisation, which has a significant impact on the value of the investment.
- Political interference or regulation changes in the industry curtail the activities and profitability of the organisation.
- A substitute competitor is not recognised in time and this competitor is able to take substantial market shares.
- These huge organisations have often leveraged funding in the form of loans, bonds or equity – if these sources of finance fail to continue to support the group it will be forced to divest in assets.
- The placement of poor leadership in the corporate organisations which, if inadequately monitored, leads to a performance downturn in a significant part of the organisation.

SUMMARY

Changing an organisations design is always a risk and should not be undertaken lightly.

An organisation that moves too quickly into a higher level of organisation design will increase its costs, which will weaken its performance and could lead to failure. Alternatively, moving too slowly to a higher model increases the potential for the organisation to be constrained by its design, possibly losing market share to competitors that are more flexible and have an organisation design aligned to the complexities of its stakeholder needs.

All of these models have weaknesses that the model above it addresses; this is the main reason why organisations want to move to a more complex model as it will enable growth. The benefit of growth is that an organisation ought to have more resources to protect it from market downturns or internal crisis risks and this brings stability to the business that in turn attracts more investors.

213

The common theme of why the organisations fail tends to be the quality of its leadership, not the design. The design is an enabler of a strategy but it is only one of many factors that will dictate whether a strategy is successful. This means that the choice of design and whether it is a good one may only be seen in hindsight.

An organisation design is appropriate at a point in time for an organisation. As the organisation and/or its environment changes, it is likely that the design will also have to adapt. The bottom line for a design is whether it takes the organisation forward from where it is and whether it will support the competitiveness of the organisation.

"In today's world a good organisation design is one that lasts long enough to get you to the next one. A continuously changing business environment requires a continuously changing organisation design to keep pace." Jay R. Galbraith, *Designing Organisations*, page 135, Jossey-Bass, 2002.

RECOMMENDED READING

I have been influenced by many theorists and business leaders while developing the ideas introduced in this book. If you would like to read more, below is a list of books that elaborate on organisation design and work complexity.

A MORE COMPLEX WORLD

The world is becoming increasingly complex, leading to more complex work and a need for new models of society and organisations. To understand the context and speed of this change the following books are recommended:

Future Shock and *The Third Wave* by Alvin Toffler (Pan)
These books provide an insight into understanding how the world is changing as it becomes more complex and moves into knowledge-based work. The books cover a huge scope of subjects in an analysis of the impact of change on societies.

Blood Sweat and Tears – The Evolution of Work by Richard Donkin (Texere)
This is a history of work and how it has changed over the centuries. It provides an excellent overview of how industrial/business work is becoming more complex and global.

Executive Leadership – A Practical Guide to Managing Complexity by Elliot Jaques and Stephen D. Clement Cason (Hall & Co)
This is one of the core texts to understanding the concept of how work can be categorised into different bands of complexity. From an appreciation of complexity bands, Jaques expands the theory of how an organisation should be structured for effective performance and leadership.

The World is Flat by Thomas L. Friedman (Penguin Books)
This book details changes in a globalised world.

MANAGING ORGANISATIONS

There are hundreds of books detailing management, human resources and other processes found in organisations. Two of the most useful books on this subject are:

Working in Organisations by Andrew Kakabadse, Ron Ludlow and Susan Vinnicombe (Penguin Business)

Understanding Organisations by Charles Handy (Penguin)

DESIGNING ORGANISATIONS

The design of organisations needs to deliver the work its stakeholders want. The world of work has been changing rapidly with new technology, knowledge and globalisation. Some of the books that will help to understand these changes on designs are:

Designing Effective Organisations by Michael Goold and Andrew Campbell (Jossey-Bass)

Competing by Design by David A. Nadler and Michael L. Tushman (Oxford University Press)

Organisation Design by Naomi Stanford (The Economist)

Organisation Design by Richard M. Burton, Gerardine DeSanctis and Borge Obel (Cambridge)

One of the most prolific writers on organisation design is Jay R. Galbraith. Some of his more enlightening books are:

Designing Organisations – An Executive Guide to Strategy, Structure and Process (Jossey-Bass)

Designing Your Organisation – Using the Star Model to Solve

Critical Design Challenges, co-authored with Amy Kates (Jossey-Bass)

Designing Dynamic Organisations, co-authored with Amy Kates and Diane Downey (Amacom)

Designing Organizations: An Executive Guide to Strategy, Structure, and Process, Revised 2nd Edition by Jay R. Galbraith (Pfeiffer)

INDEX

223

226

[Created with **TExtract** / www.Texyz.
    com]

www.ingramcontent.com/pod-product-compliance
Lightning Source LLC
Chambersburg PA
CBHW061727270326
41928CB00011B/2143